OWEN McCAFFERTY

Born in 1961, Owen lives with his wife and three children
in Belfast. His work includes *Shoot the Crow* (Druid, Galway,
1997; Royal Exchange, Manchester, 2003); *Mojo Mickybo*
(Kabosh, Belfast, 1998); *No Place Like Home* (Tinderbox,
Belfast, 2001); and *Closing Time* (National Theatre, 2002).

Other Titles from Nick Hern Books

Howard Brenton
55 DAYS
#AIWW: THE ARREST OF AI WEIWEI
ANNE BOLEYN
BERLIN BERTIE
DANCES OF DEATH
FAUST – PARTS ONE & TWO
    after Goethe
IN EXTREMIS
NEVER SO GOOD
PAUL
THE RAGGED TROUSERED
    PHILANTHROPISTS *after* Tressell

Jez Butterworth
JERUSALEM
JEZ BUTTERWORTH PLAYS: ONE
MOJO
THE NIGHT HERON
PARLOUR SONG
THE RIVER
THE WINTERLING

Alexi Kaye Campbell
APOLOGIA
BRACKEN MOOR
THE FAITH MACHINE
THE PRIDE

Caryl Churchill
BLUE HEART
CHURCHILL PLAYS: THREE
CHURCHILL PLAYS: FOUR
CHURCHILL: SHORTS
CLOUD NINE
DING DONG THE WICKED
A DREAM PLAY *after* Strindberg
DRUNK ENOUGH TO SAY
    I LOVE YOU?
FAR AWAY
HOTEL
ICECREAM
LIGHT SHINING IN
    BUCKINGHAMSHIRE
LOVE AND INFORMATION
MAD FOREST
A NUMBER
SEVEN JEWISH CHILDREN
THE SKRIKER
THIS IS A CHAIR
THYESTES *after* Seneca
TRAPS

David Edgar
ALBERT SPEER
ARTHUR & GEORGE *after* Barnes
CONTINENTAL DIVIDE
DR JEKYLL AND MR HYDE
    after R.L. Stevenson
EDGAR: SHORTS
IF ONLY
THE MASTER BUILDER *after* Ibsen
PENTECOST
PLAYING WITH FIRE
THE PRISONER'S DILEMMA
THE SHAPE OF THE TABLE
TESTING THE ECHO
A TIME TO KEEP *with* Stephanie Dale
WRITTEN ON THE HEART

Stella Feehily
BANG BANG BANG
DREAMS OF VIOLENCE
DUCK
O GO MY MAN

Debbie Tucker Green
BORN BAD
DIRTY BUTTERFLY
RANDOM
STONING MARY
TRADE & GENERATIONS
TRUTH AND RECONCILIATION

Tony Kushner
ANGELS IN AMERICA –
    PARTS ONE AND TWO
CAROLINE, OR CHANGE
HOMEBODY/KABUL

Liz Lochhead
BLOOD AND ICE
DRACULA *after* Bram Stoker
EDUCATING AGNES ('The School
    for Wives') *after* Molière
GOOD THINGS
LIZ LOCHHEAD: FIVE PLAYS
MARY QUEEN OF SCOTS GOT
    HER HEAD CHOPPED OFF
MEDEA *after* Euripides
MISERYGUTS & TARTUFFE
    after Molière
PERFECT DAYS
THEBANS

Owen McCafferty
ANTIGONE *after* Sophocles
CLOSING TIME
COLD COMFORT
DAYS OF WINE AND ROSES
MOJO MICKYBO
SHOOT THE CROW

Conor McPherson
DUBLIN CAROL
McPHERSON: FOUR PLAYS
McPHERSON PLAYS: TWO
McPHERSON PLAYS: THREE
THE NIGHT ALIVE
PORT AUTHORITY
THE SEAFARER
SHINING CITY
THE VEIL
THE WEIR

Enda Walsh
BEDBOUND & MISTERMAN
DELIRIUM
DISCO PIGS & SUCKING DUBLIN
ENDA WALSH PLAYS: ONE
MISTERMAN
THE NEW ELECTRIC BALLROOM
ONCE
PENELOPE
THE SMALL THINGS
THE WALWORTH FARCE

Tom Wells
JUMPERS FOR GOALPOSTS
THE KITCHEN SINK
ME, AS A PENGUIN

Owen McCafferty

SCENES FROM
THE BIG PICTURE

NICK HERN BOOKS
London
www.nickhernbooks.co.uk

A Nick Hern Book

This edition first published in Great Britain in 2003 as a paperback original by Nick Hern Books Limited, The Glasshouse, 49a Goldhawk Road, London W12 8QP

Reprinted 2013

Cover photo: Getty Images

Typeset by Country Setting, Kingsdown, Kent CT14 8ES
Printed in Great Britain by Bookmarque, Croydon, Surrey

ISBN 978 1 85459 729 8

A CIP catalogue record for this book is available from the British Library

FOR PEGGY

Scenes from the Big Picture was first performed in the Cottesloe
Theatre, Royal National Theatre, London, on 10 April 2003.
The cast, in order of speaking, was as follows:

BOP TORBETT	Darren Healy
MAGGIE LYTTLE	Elaine Cassidy
MAEVE HYNES	Aoife McMahon
JOE HYNES	Patrick O'Kane
SAMMY LENNON	John Normington
CONNIE DEAN	Kathy Kiera Clarke
BETTY LENNON	June Watson
THERESA BLACK	Frances Tomelty
DAVE BLACK	Dermot Crowley
FRANK COIN	Harry Towb
ROBBIE MULLIN	Chris Corrigan
SHANKS O'NEILL	Karl Johnson
BOBBIE TORBETT	Ron Donachie
SHARON LAWTHER	Eileen Pollock
HELEN WOODS	Michelle Fairley
PAUL FOGGARTY	Ruairi Conaghan
COOPER JONES	Gerard Jordan
SWIZ MURDOCH	Packy Lee
HARRY FOGGARTY	Stuart McQuarrie
SPILO JOHNSTON	Breffni McKenna
RAT JOYCE	Andy Moore

Director	Peter Gill
Designer	Alison Chitty
Lighting Designer	Hartley T.A. Kemp
Sound Score	Terry Davies and Rich Walsh
Company Voice Work	Patsy Rodenburg
Dialect Coach	Majella Hurley

Notes

The play takes place over the course of a hot summer's day in an imagined area of present-day Belfast.

ACT ONE, SCENE 1	The night before
ACT ONE, SCENES 2 – 12	The beginning of the day
ACT TWO	The middle of the day
ACT THREE	The end of the day

(a) whenever phone coversations are taking place the person making the call walks into the scene of the person receiving the call. The characters should speak directly to each other even though they are on the phone.

(b) There is a constant hum of the city in the air.

Characters

BOP TORBETT, *late teens*

MAGGIE LYTTLE, *mid teens*

MAEVE HYNES, *late twenties*

JOE HYNES, *mid thirties*

SAMMY LENNON, *early seventies*

CONNIE DEAN, *mid twenties*

BETTY LENNON, *late sixties*

THERESA BLACK, *mid fifties*

DAVE BLACK, *mid fifties*

FRANK COIN, *mid seventies*

ROBBIE MULLIN, *mid thirties*

SHANKS O'NEILL, *early fifties*

BOBBIE TORBETT, *early fifties*

SHARON LAWTHER, *late forties*

HELEN WOODS, *late twenties*

PAUL FOGGARTY, *early thirties*

COOPER JONES, *early twenties*

SWIZ MURDOCK, *early twenties*

HARRY FOGGARTY, *mid thirties*

SPILO JOHNSTON, *early thirties*

RAT JOYCE, *mid twenties*

ACT ONE

The beginning of day.

The stage is filled with noise. A baby crying. A busy road. Loud music. Church bells ringing. Heavy machinery. Police sirens. Gun shots. People arguing. Screaming. The noise dies.

1

The street. The middle of the night. COOPER *and* SWIZ *are breaking into the shop.* MAGGIE *and* BOP *are keeping dick.*

BOP TORBETT. this is dankers – mon we'll shift

MAGGIE LYTTLE. a told cooper i'd wait – he'll gurn if a don't.

BOP TORBETT. they're just in there for the want of somethin to do it is

MAGGIE LYTTLE. stop brickin it

BOP TORBETT. everything's hassle – that fight at the club tonight – there'll be trouble about that – the druggie guy's a balloon

MAGGIE LYTTLE. a saw him an swiz's brother rantin in each other's faces

BOP TORBETT. swiz's brother's a bloodnut – think a might give it a miss from now on

MAGGIE LYTTLE. see the guy with his head lyin open – blood all over the place

BOP TORBETT. nah i was in the thick of it with cooper an swiz tryin to sort things out

MAGGIE LYTTLE. were ya

BOP TORBETT. yeah – a was

MAGGIE LYTTLE. too many headbins there – a don't want to go back to school thinkin i've spent the whole summer with them

BOP TORBETT. school – loose that lot a guff

MAGGIE LYTTLE. no bop that's right – i'll do what you do – nothin

BOP TORBETT. not nothin – i don't do nothin

MAGGIE LYTTLE. nothin multiplied by itself ya do

BOP TORBETT. gonna get a job in the meat plant – bop the meat man – that's not nothin

MAGGIE LYTTLE. shootin cows an cuttin the throats a pigs all day long – what would ya want that for

BOP TORBETT. do alright – get some spondulix maggie y'know

MAGGIE LYTTLE. couldn't picture myself doing somethin forever

BOP TORBETT. forever what – end up like my da – worked there an now has nothin – it's a starter that's all

MAGGIE LYTTLE. look – look – ya see that – look

BOP TORBETT. what – someone comin

MAGGIE LYTTLE. up in the sky ya tool – a shootin star or somethin it was

BOP TORBETT. where

MAGGIE LYTTLE. it's away now – ya ever just look up at the stars

BOP TORBETT. nah

MAGGIE LYTTLE. i sit in the yard sometimes an look up at the sky – you should do that

BOP TORBETT. why

MAGGIE LYTTLE. why do ya need a reason – ya should do it that's all

BOP TORBETT. aye

MAGGIE LYTTLE. ya should

BOP TORBETT. must make a note of that – look up at the stars at night

MAGGIE LYTTLE. don't be an arse meat boy

BOP TORBETT. don't be sayin meat boy to them a don't want them slabberin

MAGGIE LYTTLE. you worry too much bop – mon me an you'll do somethin tomorrow

BOP TORBETT. like what

MAGGIE LYTTLE. like anythin – something different – get away out a here for a day

BOP TORBETT. away out a here where

MAGGIE LYTTLE. somewhere – we'll go swimmin up by the river other side of the park

BOP TORBETT. can't swim

MAGGIE LYTTLE. bop can't swim – who'd a thought (*She kisses him.*)

BOP TORBETT. what ya do that for

MAGGIE LYTTLE. cause you can't swim – why ya not like it

BOP TORBETT. a did – just want to know why

MAGGIE LYTTLE. cause a like ya – you're a sweetie that can't swim

BOP TORBETT. what about cooper

MAGGIE LYTTLE. what about him – is he here – a told ya stop brickin yerself all the time – ya want to go swimmin with me or not

BOP TORBETT. do ya not have to be able to swim in order to go swimmin

MAGGIE LYTTLE. i'll teach ya – i'm a fish – i'll teach ya to be a fish – a fish an a meat boy

BOP TORBETT. swimmin in a river – aye dead on

MAGGIE LYTTLE. ya can watch me then

BOP TORBETT. what about cooper

MAGGIE LYTTLE. shut up

BOP TORBETT. he'll give me grief

MAGGIE LYTTLE. i think ya should go – ya might enjoy it

BOP TORBETT. aye alright but i'm not gettin in

MAGGIE LYTTLE. i'll teach ya to be a fish

BOP TORBETT. why do ya want me to go

MAGGIE LYTTLE. shut up – don't ask questions all the time

BOP TORBETT. i'll shut up then (*Breaking glass in the shop.*)
    what the fuck was that – am not stayin here – leave them
    two – i'll walk ya home – mon

MAGGIE LYTTLE. i'm waitin on cooper a told ya that

BOP TORBETT. am goin well

MAGGIE LYTTLE. away ya go then

2

A house. The kitchen. JOE *is sitting at a table having a cup
of tea.* MAEVE *is at the counter making his lunch.*

MAEVE HYNES. cheese do ya – there is nothin else anyway
    has to be cheese – too much meat bad for ya

JOE HYNES. a thought we only had cheese

MAEVE HYNES. we do – need to keep you healthy – virile

JOE HYNES. aye cheese – not get time to eat it anyway

MAEVE HYNES. why am a makin it then

JOE HYNES. i'm only sayin a mightn't

MAEVE HYNES. shouldn't be workin without eatin

JOE HYNES. a won't

MAEVE HYNES. not good for ya

JOE HYNES. a just said a won't – be meetins all day instead a graftin – listenin to the same shit an then havin to report the whole bloody thing

MAEVE HYNES. a told ya not to take it on it's a thankless bloody task

JOE HYNES. none a the rest would do it

MAEVE HYNES. the have more sense that's why

JOE HYNES. the asked me – that means somethin

MAEVE HYNES. the asked ya because the didn't want it – an you fell for it – shopsteward – somethin happens you'll be the first to go

JOE HYNES. ya goin up to the hospital again today

MAEVE HYNES. ya know i am

JOE HYNES. ya should go back to work – they'll not hold the job open forever

MAEVE HYNES. a know – i'll go back – just not right now that's all – julie needs me at the moment – that's important – she has no one – ya know that joe

JOE HYNES. yes maeve i understand she has no one – it's just

MAEVE HYNES. it's just what

JOE HYNES. you know what

MAEVE HYNES. a don't know what tell me – a cousin a mine's havin a baby – might even be today – she has no one – i'm there – so – tell me

JOE HYNES. the timin of it – that's all – the timin of the whole situation doesn't seem spot on does it

MAEVE HYNES. what situation – if ya think i'm goin crazy joe just say it

JOE HYNES. stop talkin like that maeve – that's not what a mean an ya know it

MAEVE HYNES. it feels like that to me

JOE HYNES. alright – for whatever reasons and nobody's quite sure about that yet

MAEVE HYNES. no they're not

JOE HYNES. for whatever reasons the doctor tells ya it's unlikely yer gonna be able to have kids

MAEVE HYNES. a know that – don't tell me things a know

JOE HYNES. don't go into one here again

MAEVE HYNES. just tell me why i'm goin crazy joe

JOE HYNES. stop sayin that – the tell ya that right – next thing some kid cousin a yers – who ya didn't give a monkey's about beforehand – had problems with her pregnancy an she's fired into hospital – now yer up there everyday

MAEVE HYNES. an what are ya sayin

JOE HYNES. that's what i'm sayin – it mightn't be good for ya to be hangin around there all the time – that's all i'm sayin

MAEVE HYNES. she's a kid – she's havin a baby – i'm lookin out for her – that's all – why can't you see that as a good thing

JOE HYNES. yer right – it's a good thing yer right – i'm wrong – forget i even fuckin spoke about it – do whatever ya have to do

MAEVE HYNES. a will – this about us – this is about us isn't it

JOE HYNES. it's not about us maeve

MAEVE HYNES. it is isn't it

JOE HYNES. no

MAEVE HYNES. whenever we were told that news i think you were glad

JOE HYNES. how was a glad

MAEVE HYNES. glad we mightn't have kids

JOE HYNES. what the fuck would a be glad about that for

MAEVE HYNES. why don't you talk to me about what the doctor says then – there's various treatments we could go for – you don't want to talk about that

JOE HYNES. i don't have to – you never stop talking about it

MAEVE HYNES. you don't talk about it though

JOE HYNES. maeve i've to go to work soon – i'm paid to hump meat but when a go in today i'm goin to get grief – so not now – none of this now

MAEVE HYNES. ya don't want it to happen – i know ya don't

JOE HYNES. this has to do with money – that's what this is all about – money

MAEVE HYNES. forget about it – a don't want to talk about it now – go on to work – go hump meat

JOE HYNES. nothing's secure – we can't make plans

MAEVE HYNES. that's what you say it is that's what it is

JOE HYNES. that is what it is

MAEVE HYNES. leave it then

JOE HYNES. right

MAEVE HYNES. ya want one round or two

JOE HYNES. one'll do – no two – no fegs today i'll probably eat more

MAEVE HYNES. you stickin to it

JOE HYNES. that's what we agreed isn't it

MAEVE HYNES. you'll be better off for it

JOE HYNES. increase the sperm count

3

The shop. SAMMY *is sweeping up glass.*

SAMMY LENNON. bastards – no good bloody reason – destruction that's all it is

   CONNIE DEAN *enters. She is nervey.*

watch yer feet on that glass there – see what they're doin to me – smash the bloody place up – no good reason y'know – full a drugs – wouldn't have happened years ago – destruction that's all it is – is there somethin yer lookin for dear

CONNIE DEAN. a don't know

SAMMY LENNON. ya don't know what it is yer lookin for

CONNIE DEAN. chocolate an nuts that's what a want ya do that

SAMMY LENNON. for cookin ya mean

CONNIE DEAN. no – sweets – a bar of chocolate an nuts – a big bar of chocolate with nuts in it – two big bars

SAMMY LENNON. you alright

CONNIE DEAN. three a them – three big bars – do ya have that do ya

SAMMY LENNON. it's there in front a ya

CONNIE DEAN. there's only two here

SAMMY LENNON. that's all there is – waitin on an order comin in

CONNIE DEAN. two'll do

SAMMY LENNON. five thirty eight dear

CONNIE DEAN. money yeah (*Hands him money.*) thank you

SAMMY LENNON (*at till*). clear all the bloody glass up (CONNIE *exits.*) new windows an that – (*Turns.*) yer change – here – what the hell is up with people

SAMMY *goes back to sweeping.* BETTY *enters with two cups of tea.*

what's wrong with this place – she just walked out without her change – people can hardly talk ya know that

BETTY LENNON. here drink yer tea

SAMMY LENNON. bet ya she was on bloody drugs too – this time a day – meant to be startin yer day's work not takin bloody drugs

BETTY LENNON. just drink yer tea sammy

SAMMY LENNON. aye drink my tea – look at the bloody glass everywhere

BETTY LENNON. we'll clear it up

SAMMY LENNON. aye – clear it up – sell the bloody place – we're gettin too old for this game betty dear

BETTY LENNON. who'd a thought i'd end up stuck with an old man

SAMMY LENNON. only three years of a difference

BETTY LENNON. five years – not three – five

SAMMY LENNON. i thought it was three

BETTY LENNON. no ya didn't – you know fine rightly

SAMMY LENNON. ya should've stayed in bed – get a bit more rest

BETTY LENNON. don't fuss sammy

SAMMY LENNON. i'm not fussin – a bit a rest that's all

BETTY LENNON. a slept well enough

SAMMY LENNON. there's nothin to worry about

BETTY LENNON. a know that

SAMMY LENNON. it's only a check up – the hospital said it's only a check up didn't the

BETTY LENNON. don't fuss

SAMMY LENNON. that's what the said though isn't it

BETTY LENNON. yes sammy that's what the said – it's fine

SAMMY LENNON. do you want me to go with ya

BETTY LENNON. no – no a don't – fussin round me – there's an order this afternoon you can't close the shop up

SAMMY LENNON. get a taxi

BETTY LENNON. i'll get a taxi

SAMMY LENNON. a don't like ya in taxis

BETTY LENNON. sammy stop it – it's fine – did ya phone the police yet

SAMMY LENNON. what bloody good did it do the last time – and the time before that – i've had enough – why don't we sell the damn place

BETTY LENNON. that doesn't stop us phonin the police

SAMMY LENNON. a don't want them involved – keep comin back here askin the same damn questions – makes me feel like a fool – a fool that can't look after his own business

BETTY LENNON. people don't think like that sammy

BETTY LENNON. protect ourselves that's what we're goin to be doin

BETTY LENNON. how are we goin to do that

SAMMY LENNON. beat the hell out a them that's what i'd like to do

BETTY LENNON. now you do sound like a fool

SAMMY LENNON. we'll get an alarm system – there's a bit of money put aside – get one that electrocutes them

Door bell rings.

(*To customer.*) watch the glass there – what can a do for ya

4

A house. The living room. THERESA *is putting make-up on to go out. She is dressed in black for a funeral.* DAVE *has spent the night in the armchair.*

THERESA BLACK. sleepin in that armchair put yer back out

DAVE BLACK. a didn't sleep – tried a few a them tablets a yers – useless

THERESA BLACK. you have to want to sleep for them to work – ya had any breakfast yet

DAVE BLACK. sort somethin out later

THERESA BLACK. this look alright

DAVE BLACK. it's fine

DAVE BLACK. not too tight

DAVE BLACK. fine – over the top for the meat plant like

THERESA BLACK. i've to go to a funeral

DAVE BLACK. a funeral

THERESA BLACK. yeah a know

DAVE BLACK. anybody we know

THERESA BLACK. some guy used to work there – before my time

DAVE BLACK. a funeral – today

THERESA BLACK. masters is away i've to go on his behalf – better nip into the office before a go to the church see if he's left me any messages – leaves everything to the last minute then i've to sort it all out

DAVE BLACK. the amount of time ya spend there i'm sure it's under control

THERESA BLACK. don't start

DAVE BLACK. i'm not – i'm just tired

THERESA BLACK. you should've slept

DAVE BLACK. a couldn't – you did though

THERESA BLACK. a thought ya weren't goin to start

DAVE BLACK. i'm not

THERESA BLACK. i've had sleepless nights

DAVE BLACK. a know – i'm sorry – the abattoir closin for the day

THERESA BLACK. more chance of me goin out with no make up on

DAVE BLACK. he doesn't like losin money that boy

THERESA BLACK. he's down the south chasin business – if he doesn't get this contract i don't know what's goin to happen – i've to deal with it all too – not knowin what's goin to happen – it shouldn't be my job dealin with that

DAVE BLACK. tell him that

THERESA BLACK. he'd only start up about how pushed he is tryin to keep the whole thing goin

DAVE BLACK. you don't owe him anythin – a day's work for a day's pay

THERESA BLACK. i know that

DAVE BLACK. no control over anythin – that's what's wrong with us – no control – does the rest a them know what's happenin

THERESA BLACK. he won't let me tell

DAVE BLACK. don't lie for him theresa

THERESA BLACK. i'm not – a wouldn't

DAVE BLACK. none of it's worth it – none of it's worth a fuck

THERESA BLACK. we have to work dave our situation doesn't change that

DAVE BLACK. our situation changes everything

THERESA BLACK. why don't ya get ready for work

DAVE BLACK. i'm not goin to work

THERESA BLACK. what about the job yer on

DAVE BLACK. fixin a few tiles on some woman's roof – what – i'm puttin things into perspective here – my boy's lyin in the cold earth somewhere – he's been lyin there for fifteen years – it's time we found him

THERESA BLACK. our boy – not yers – ours

DAVE BLACK. yes – our boy

THERESA BLACK. they're lookin dave – they've been lookin for months – they've ripped the countryside up – what more is there to do

DAVE BLACK. and today's the day they're goin to stop – i think we should be doin something – makin them not stop – not stop until the find him an we can be allowed to bury him – bury him so the fuckers that shot him don't have the last say

THERESA BLACK. if the haven't found thomas by now dave the won't

DAVE BLACK. the will if the don't stop – i'm not lettin this be the last day

THERESA BLACK. go to work

DAVE BLACK. no – somethin has to be done

THERESA BLACK. what

DAVE BLACK. a don't know – it's funny yer dressed for someone's funeral and the one thing we want is a funeral of our own

THERESA BLACK. it's not funny

DAVE BLACK. i think it is

THERESA BLACK. i'll pick up somethin to eat on the way to work

DAVE BLACK. it's alright – it is – it's alright

THERESA BLACK (*kisses him.*) a know that

DAVE BLACK. i'll phone ya

THERESA BLACK. i'll be busy

DAVE BLACK. i'll phone ya any way

THERESA BLACK. why don't you go an get dressed

DAVE BLACK. a will – i will

5

A house. FRANK COIN *is tying his shoe laces. The radio is on.*

RADIO. and the political talks continue although all parties involved have agreed they have reached an impasse – and finally – on the business front the euro has again dropped against the pound and the dollar.

FRANK *turns the radio off.*

FRANK COIN. another day ahead of us elsie – go out here and stretch my legs.

6

A flat. CONNIE *is looking out the window.* ROBBIE *is counting pills and putting them in plastic bags.*

ROBBIE MULLIN. we need more bags – did i not ask you to check this

CONNIE DEAN. no – the sun's shinin – fills the street with colour it does

ROBBIE MULLIN. a did ask ya didn't a

CONNIE DEAN. no robbie ya didn't – you want me to go out an get some

ROBBIE MULLIN. i'll get them later

CONNIE DEAN. can we go somewhere today – a drive or somethin

ROBBIE MULLIN. no

CONNIE DEAN. why not

ROBBIE MULLIN. stop talkin i'm tryin to count these – just keep lookin out the window

CONNIE DEAN. there's no one there – a want to have a bath

ROBBIE MULLIN. stand there

CONNIE DEAN. there's no one there

ROBBIE MULLIN. shut up

Silence. ROBBIE *counts.*

you looked well last night – did a tell ya that

CONNIE DEAN. no

ROBBIE MULLIN. well ya did – a like it when ya look well

CONNIE DEAN. can a have my bath then

ROBBIE MULLIN. no just keep lookin

CONNIE DEAN. was last night bad robbie

ROBBIE MULLIN. the tried to wire me off an a told them to go fuck themselves – yeah it's bad – fuckin punks the are – more money they're lookin – squarin up to them's always bad – the don't like losin face – it's fucked – we're goin to have to split

CONNIS DEAN. leave the flat

ROBBIE MULLIN. yeah leave the flat

CONNIE DEAN. i like it here

ROBBIE MULLIN. the don't like bein fucked over – that means somethin's goin to happen

CONNIE DEAN. where we goin to go then

ROBBIE MULLIN. what's that matter to you – you've fuck all else place to go

CONNIE DEAN. i could live on my own – make my own way

ROBBIE MULLIN. some poxy fuckin bedsit whorin for a pill

CONNIE DEAN. i'm not a whore – and it wouldn't be a bedsit

ROBBIE MULLIN. what would it be – a fuckin palace

CONNIE DEAN. there's a man just parked his car across the street

ROBBIE MULLIN *(at window).* where

CONNIE DEAN. there across the street

ROBBIE MULLIN. nah – never seen him before – too well dressed anyway that guy – (*He kisses her and feels her breasts then moves away.*) this might work out alright

CONNIE DEAN. he's away down the street anyway

ROBBIE MULLIN. ya can be doin somethin an just get stuck in it – somethin needs to happen – dealin with scumbags – who are the – fuckin nobodies – wee bits here wee bits there – gettin nurses with fuck all to steal gear from the hospital – fuck that

CONNIE DEAN. ya know nothin else

ROBBIE MULLIN. a don't want to have to deal with lowlife scumbags any more – the fuckers would sell their children for a bag a pills – go up market – expand the business – start dealin with people that has a bit a money about them – and by the way there's plenty a fuckin things i could do – wouldn't suit you anyway if a was to run a fuckin bike shop or somethin would it

CONNIE DEAN. i could help out – there's things i could do

ROBBIE MULLIN. like what connie

CONNIE DEAN. can't think now don't ask me now

ROBBIE MULLIN. people who help out aren't fucked out a their heads half the time – make me a nice dinner after a come home from a hard day at the bike shop maybe – look after the kids – at the end a the day sort out the accounts – deal with the vat man

CONNIE DEAN. i'm not useless robbie

ROBBIE MULLIN. nobody said you were useless – yer just too used to this

CONNIE DEAN. why do you talk to me like that – a don't like it

ROBBIE MULLIN. i don't like havin to deal with lowlife fuckweeds all the time – ya want somethin to eat

CONNIE DEAN. a want a bath

ROBBIE MULLIN. what's in the kitchen

CONNIE DEAN. bread maybe – there's chocolate there

ROBBIE MULLIN. chocolate for breakfast

CONNIE DEAN. buy some food when yer gettin the bags

ROBBIE MULLIN. chocolate – where'd that come from anyway

CONNIE DEAN. i bought it the other day

ROBBIE MULLIN. the other day when – were you out

CONNIE DEAN. no – the other day it was – you were with me

ROBBIE MULLIN. i can't remember that

CONNIE DEAN. ya were there

ROBBIE MULLIN. don't lie to me

CONNIE DEAN. ya were there

ROBBIE MULLIN. right – bread – fuck – ya want a cup a tea

CONNIE DEAN. no

ROBBIE MULLIN. i'll make some anyway – keep lookin out the window

7

A house. The parlour. BOBBIE *and* SHANKS *are dressed for a funeral.* SHANKS *is drinking a tin of beer.* SHARON *and* BOP *are upstairs.*

SHANKS O'NEILL. ya spoken to her this mornin

BOBBIE TORBETT. she hasn't surfaced yet

SHANKS O'NEILL. she kip up there

BOBBIE TORBETT. aye

SHANKS O'NEILL. in yer scratcher

BOBBIE TORBETT. aye – didn't get me eyes shut all night

SHANKS O'NEILL. you an her givin it all that other message

BOBBIE TORBETT. a was on the sofa – not gettin involved in all that caper

SHANKS O'NEILL. a just thought ya might have slipped one in for old time's sake

BOBBIE TORBETT. lyin on that has my back wrecked

SHANKS O'NEILL. she still not bad lookin – she was always alright with the make up on

BOBBIE TORBETT. doesn't matter how she looks i'm not getting involved

SHANKS O'NEILL. an ole ride's an ole ride all the same

BOBBIE TORBETT. she's a rocket

SHANKS O'NEILL. she likes you though

BOBBIE TORBETT. still a rocket

SHANKS O'NEILL. blocked was she

BOBBIE TORBETT. all over the show – cryin – huggin – all that fuckin gear

SHANKS O'NEILL. turfed out

BOBBIE TORBETT. that's what she said

SHANKS O'NEILL. who's she with now

BOBBIE TORBETT. don't know – couldn't make any sense of her

SHANKS O'NEILL. she's weighed in blocked an he's turfed her out

BOBBIE TORBETT. aye

SHANKS O'NEILL. ya should've give her one

BOBBIE TORBETT. a don't want to get involved again

SHANKS O'NEILL. she wouldn't have remembered anything about it – a freebie

BOBBIE TORBETT. what an the wee lad in the next room – fuck that – that's not the point anyway

SHANKS O'NEILL. that her handbag

BOBBIE TORBETT. no it's mine – don't be at that caper

SHANKS O'NEILL. what (*Opens bag.*) a few quid gets ya a
starter for the day

BOBBIE TORBETT. yer a tosspot

SHANKS O'NEILL (*closes bag*). a tosspot with a tenner in his
skyrocket – you'll not refuse a pint out of it

BOBBIE TORBETT. you buy a pint – aye

SHANKS O'NEILL. a buy plenty

BOBBIE TORBETT. aye

SHANKS O'NEILL. get a few pints at this funeral

BOBBIE TORBETT. wee foggarty – one old fucker – couldn't
bury him deep enough

SHANKS O'NEILL. his sons be at it – they'd be good for a
few pints

BOBBIE TORBETT. the don't speak – the sons don't speak

SHANKS O'NEILL. double dunter – pint from one – pint
from the other – fuckin sweet

BOBBIE TORBETT. what will a say to yer woman

SHANKS O'NEILL. tell her to follow us round after the
funeral

BOBBIE TORBETT. what for

SHANKS O'NEILL. bit of a laugh

BOBBIE TORBETT. fuckin sure am not

BOP *enters. He is just out of bed.*

BOP TORBETT. who's up the stairs – couldn't sleep with the
snores a them

SHANKS O'NEILL. should be up at the crack a dawn yer age

BOP TORBETT. drink yer tin

SHANKS O'NEILL. out all hours – chasin it – up some entry
with a wee doll

BOBBIE TORBETT. drink yer tin – there's a letter there for ya

BOP TORBETT. a know a got it – who's up the stairs

BOBBIE TORBETT. member yer woman sharon – good while back it was

BOP TORBETT. the rocket

BOBBIE TORBETT. aye – she had a bit of a bad night – had to put her head down somewhere that's all

BOP TORBETT. she's not stayin

SHANKS O'NEILL. unless yer da takes a fancy to her again

BOBBIE TORBETT. you want slapped – no she's not stayin

BOP TORBETT. she's not sayin

BOBBIE TORBETT. a just said that

BOP TORBETT. i'm sayin no matter what she's not stayin

BOBBIE TORBETT. never tell me what to do – i say who stays an goes – what was the letter about

BOP TORBETT. applied for a job down in the abattoir

SHANKS O'NEILL. meat man like yer da

BOBBIE TORBETT. a job down there

BOP TORBETT. the knocked me back

BOBBIE TORBETT. there's other jobs

BOP TORBETT. it would've been handy

SHANKS O'NEILL. toughens ya up that type a work – when we're at the funeral bobbie ya could say somethin to somebody

BOBBIE TORBETT. say what

SHANKS O'NEILL. put a good word in for him

BOP TORBETT. will ya do that

BOBBIE TORBETT. the ones i know mightn't be there

SHANKS O'NEILL. they'll all be there

BOP TORBETT. will ya ask for me

BOBBIE TORBETT. i'll say somethin

BOP TORBETT. ya will

BOBBIE TORBETT. aye

BOP TORBETT. am away back to my bed

BOBBIE TORBETT. back to bed – get up there an get dressed

SHANKS O'NEILL. if he's goin to be humpin meat he needs his rest – the poor child

BOBBIE TORBETT. get yerself dressed

SHARON *enters*. BOP *is exiting*.

SHARON LAWTHER. good mornin – do ya remember me – sharon – it's a while back now – ya must remember me

BOP TORBETT. aye – ya alright (*He exits*.)

SHARON LAWTHER. the grow up quick don't the – lovely wee lad ya have bobbie – makes me think a wouldn't have minded havin children myself

BOBBIE TORBETT. he's alright – ya know shanks don't ya

SHARON LAWTHER. certainly a do – it's not that long ago we were together bobbie ya know

BOBBIE TORBETT. it's a right while

SHARON LAWTHER. not that long

SHANKS O'NEILL. bobbie was tellin me things weren't the best for ya last night – a bit a bother

BOBBIE TORBETT. sharon we're just headin out to a funeral an that

SHANKS O'NEILL. we've time yet

SHARON LAWTHER. the bastard threw me out – havin a few drinks – next thing it's all nasty pills – nasty wee fucker he can be – never hit me like – looked like he might a done last night though – that's why a came round here

BOBBIE TORBETT. it's not a situation a want to get involved with sharon

SHARON LAWTHER. but ya wouldn't let him hit me bobbie

BOBBIE TORBETT. no a wouldn't

SHARON LAWTHER. that's why a came round here bobbie cause a knew you'd look after me

BOBBIE TORBETT. he'll still be there will he

SHARON LAWTHER. might be – don't know – nasty wee bastard – wouldn't get me behavin like that – few drinks alright – there's no harm in that – a bit of a laugh

SHANKS O'NEILL. that's all we're at isn't it sharon – a few gargles an a wee bit of a laugh

SHARON LAWTHER. that's right shanks – no harm in it

BOBBIE TORBETT. ya goin round to see him then – get it sorted out

SHARON LAWTHER. a don't want to be speakin with him

SHANKS O'NEILL. just right – the dirty fucker

BOBBIE TORBETT. aye a know dirty fucker – but ya have to sort it out ya understand that

SHARON LAWTHER. wantin rid a me already

BOBBIE TORBETT. we've to go to this funeral ya see – that's what am sayin

SHARON LAWTHER. sure you go on – don't be worryin about me – i'll have a cup a tea – straighten myself out a bit then i'll go round to him – tell him if he ever pulls that stunt again me an him's finished – you go on i'll be alright

BOBBIE TORBETT. you'll lock up

SHARON LAWTHER. a know my way around bobbie – i'll have a cup of tea an i'll lock up – don't be worryin about me – where will yas be after the funeral – just in case somethin happens with him – where will yas be

BOBBIE TORBETT. ya wouldn't know where we'll end up after this sharon

SHARON LAWTHER. if needs be i'll maybe look for yas then

BOBBIE TORBETT. i'm tellin ya anywhere it could be – we right – i'll get my jacket on (*He exits.*)

SHANKS O'NEILL. you'll be alright

SHARON LAWTHER. he loves me – he threw me out but he loves me

SHANKS O'NEILL. wouldn't doubt it for a minute – i'd say after this funeral we'll end up in the tavern – if yer stuck that's where we'll be

SHARON LAWTHER. it'll be alright – bobbie look after me

SHANKS O'NEILL. course he will – we both will

BOBBIE *enters*.

BOBBIE TORBETT. ya right

SHANKS O'NEILL. aye

BOBBIE TORBETT. ya goin round to see him then

SHARON LAWTHER. yes

BOBBIE TORBETT. good

8

The shop. HELEN *enters*.

SAMMY LENNON. the broke in again the did – wasters – didn't see anything on the way home did ya

HELEN WOODS. no – wasn't much happenin a shut up early

SAMMY LENNON. aye – twenty regal is it

HELEN WOODS. twenty regal – a should stop shouldn't a

SAMMY LENNON. i've these patches here – they're good – take the edge of it

HELEN WOODS. need the willpower as well that's the problem

SAMMY LENNON. if a could sell willpower we'd be sailin

HELEN WOODS. do you have any lighters

SAMMY LENNON. a do – no patches but a lighter – yer movin in the wrong direction

HELEN WOODS. it's a present for someone

SAMMY LENNON. not one a them cheap ones then – man or woman is it for

HELEN WOODS. a man

SAMMY LENNON. boyfriend is it

HELEN WOODS. a friend – a boyfriend yeah

SAMMY LENNON. is he as good lookin as me

HELEN WOODS. no chance

MAEVE *enters*.

SAMMY LENNON. big smoker is he

HELEN WOODS. it's the only hobby the two of us have

SAMMY LENNON. zippo – zippos are the best – the cost a few quid more but the last ya a lifetime – if ya fall out with him ya can ask for it back (*To* MAEVE.) i'll get betty down now

MAEVE HYNES. it's okay i'll wait (*To* HELEN.) hello – lovely day

HELEN WOODS. it is

SAMMY LENNON (*shouts*). – a customer – the zippos are over here (HELEN *and him move down the counter*.) there's ones there with football teams on them – that one's to do with bikes – is he into that type a thing – i'm not myself but a know people are

HELEN WOODS. more of a plain one

BETTY *enters*. HELEN *and* SAMMY *look at lighters*.

BETTY LENNON. sorry – those stairs seem to be gettin steeper every time a come down them – what can a do for ya

MAEVE HYNES. nappies – my cousin's havin a baby – today maybe – thought i'd bring her up some nappies

BETTY LENNON. a new baby – that's lovely – does she know what it is

MAEVE HYNES. no – she wanted the surprise – the hospital told her to bring nappies up – you'd think that would be the one thing there'd be plenty of wouldn't ya

BETTY LENNON. you'd wonder where the money goes – just over here

JOE is in the abattoir. He makes a call on his mobile. HELEN's phone rings. JOE walks into the scene. HELEN answers her phone.

SAMMY LENNON. you work away there i'm not goin anywhere – maybe it's him – the lighter man

HELEN WOODS. hello

JOE HYNES. well how's it goin

HELEN WOODS. it's you

JOE HYNES. you expectin someone else

HELEN WOODS. no

JOE HYNES. where are ya

HELEN WOODS. on my way to work – just called into the shop – where are you

JOE HYNES. work – fuckin pain – rest a them's cleanin up – just thought i'd give ya a bell

BETTY LENNON. these are the best a think

MAEVE HYNES. they'll do then – a was thinkin of some cream as well – you know the way sometimes the get a rash

BETTY LENNON. suda cream

JOE HYNES. you alright

HELEN WOODS. yeah

JOE HYNES. what's wrong

MAEVE HYNES. there was this baby in the ward yesterday – the size of it – tiny wee hands

SAMMY LENNON. all grow up into hoods no matter what size the start off

JOE HYNES. can ya not speak

HELEN WOODS. not really no

JOE HYNES. someone there

HELEN WOODS. that would be right

MAEVE HYNES. the have dolls the mothers practise on you'd swear the were real – cry an everything the do

JOE HYNES. who – who's there

HELEN WOODS. you'd know them alright

BETTY LENNON. a big tub or a small one

MAEVE HYNES. a big one – no point in savin pennies for things like that

JOE HYNES. maeve

HELEN WOODS. yes

JOE HYNES. fuck yer jokin – were ya talkin to her

HELEN WOODS. said hello

JOE HYNES. fuck – give me grief this mornin she did – crazy bitch – babies again

HELEN WOODS. that's very interesting

SAMMY LENNON (*to* BETTY). is the baby place up near where yer goin – (*To* MAEVE.) goin for an appointment today she is

BETTY LENNON. it's the other side a the buildin

JOE HYNES. what's she at

MAEVE HYNES. what's the name of the buildin

BETTY LENNON. a can't remember – it's just a check up – the older ya get the more the want to check up

HELEN WOODS. can't really say

JOE HYNES. ya want to talk later – i've to go to the office anyway – find out what's happenin here

HELEN WOODS. yes

JOE HYNES. right

JOE *exits*. HELEN *moves back to counter.*

SAMMY LENNON. take yer time lookin dear there's no hurry
– (*To* MAEVE.) if yer leavin it until the afternoon you an
betty could go up together – a don't like her goin up on her
own an she won't let me close the shop

MAEVE HYNES. a said i'd be up there early just in case – in
case she goes

BETTY LENNON. don't be listenin to him – i'll go up on my
own – i've told him not to fuss

MAEVE HYNES. any other day

BETTY LENNON. of course

SAMMY LENNON. anythin needed for babies we have it here
– no need to be lookin elsewhere

FRANK COIN *enters and waits to be served.*

HELEN WOODS. this one here a think

SAMMY LENNON. yer boyfriend will like that one – good
plain solid lighter – you and him hardly be at the baby stage
yet

BETTY LENNON. sammy

SAMMY LENNON. i'm only talkin – (*To* HELEN.) i'm only
talkin dear

HELEN WOODS. that's alright – no we're not at that stage yet

MAEVE HYNES. until the baby actually arrives a don't think
men have much interest in all a that

HELEN WOODS. no probably not

MAEVE HYNES. when the have them in their arms it's a
different matter

HELEN WOODS. how much is that

SAMMY LENNON. sixteen an the cigarettes – four sixty-
twenty sixty please – he'll not need to be buyin another
lighter for the rest of his days

BETTY LENNON (*to* MAEVE). that'll be six forty an two
thirty – eight seventy altogether

HELEN WOODS. better be off to my work

SAMMY LENNON. there's nothin else for it dear

HELEN WOODS (*exiting – to* FRANK). ya weren't about last night – we all thought the world had stopped

FRANK COIN. didn't a fall asleep in front of the fire – lookin forward to a pint a was too

HELEN WOODS. i'll keep ya one this evenin

FRANK COIN. my name's on it

HELEN *exits*.

SAMMY LENNON (*to* MAEVE). nice girl that – runs the pub down the way – whatever man she ends up with be lucky to get her (*To* FRANK.) the usual – a pint a milk and a few slices of chicken

FRANK COIN. that be right

MAEVE HYNES. i'll go on – hopefully haven't missed the big event

BETTY LENNON. i'm sure she'll wait

MAEVE HYNES. she's waited this long

BETTY LENNON. that's right

MAEVE *exits*.

SAMMY LENNON. two or three slices is it

FRANK COIN. two

BETTY LENNON (*to* SAMMY). don't be sayin to people about takin me anywhere

SAMMY LENNON. a don't like ya goin up there on yer own that's all

BETTY LENNON. stop bloody fussin (*To* FRANK.) how's things today

FRANK COIN. good enough – sure one day much the same as the rest

BETTY LENNON. that's right and the truer it gets the older you are

9

The abattoir. THERESA*'s office. She is on the phone.*

THERESA BLACK. i understand mr masters is at a meeting
   and can't be disturbed – what i'm tellin you is he has to be
   disturbed – yes a know only too well that you're just doin
   what you've been told – but a need to – right – right – if he
   comes out for any reason at all – tell him to phone theresa –
   it's very important – he has to phone me – right thank you
   (*Phone down.*) dosey bitch (JOE *enters.*) yes joe

JOE HYNES. what's the score here

THERESA BLACK. i'm tryin to get in contact with him – he's
   at a meetin

JOE HYNES. ya haven't spoken to him

THERESA BLACK. he left a message on the machine for me
   this mornin an all it said was – i'm waitin on the euro

JOE HYNES. the train

THERESA BLACK. the currency

JOE HYNES. what does that mean waitin on the euro – i'm
   not goin back down to tell them we're waitin on the fuckin
   euro

THERESA BLACK. that's all a know

JOE HYNES. phone him

THERESA BLACK. i've left three messages for him

JOE HYNES. waitin on the euro

THERESA BLACK. the rate of it

JOE HYNES. i know

THERESA BLACK. good rate get the best price

JOE HYNES. what happens if the rate's not good

THERESA BLACK. i know as much as you do

JOE HYNES. a have to say somethin to them

DAVE *on a busy street. Makes a call on his mobile.*
THERESA*'s phone rings.* DAVE *walks into the scene.*

THERESA BLACK. sorry joe – yes – what – i'm busy

DAVE BLACK. i'm on my way to the bbc

THERESA BLACK. what bbc – did ya not go to work

DAVE BLACK. i'm on my way to the bbc

THERESA BLACK. what for

DAVE BLACK. i'm goin on the radio

THERESA BLACK. the radio

DAVE BLACK. aye

THERESA BLACK. the get in contact with ya

DAVE BLACK. no

THERESA BLACK. i don't understand – i'm in the middle a somethin here dave

DAVE BLACK. so am i – i'm in the middle a somethin to – i'm goin round to get on the radio

THERESA BLACK. arrive an demand to go on

DAVE BLACK. that's right – there's people on the radio all the time – no reason why i shouldn't be – bring it out in the open – put pressure on them – that's the right way to do it isn't it – isn't it

THERESA BLACK. the just don't let people do that

DAVE BLACK. won't know until a try – i'm phonin to say that's what i'm doin – just in case ya hear me

THERESA BLACK. i'll hardly have time

DAVE BLACK. aye whatever – i'll phone ya later

THERESA BLACK. right

DAVE *exits.*

JOE HYNES. what am a goin to say down here

THERESA BLACK. what are ya goin to tell them

JOE HYNES. aye what am a goin to tell them – the know there's a container at the dock – the want to know why they're standin around then

THERESA BLACK. you know as much as i do

JOE HYNES. there's no problem with gettin paid is there

THERESA BLACK. there'll be wages at the end a the day

JOE HYNES. what am a goin to tell them

THERESA BLACK. tell them – tell them – tell them the meat's to be inspected at the dock – that's why we can't unload it yet

JOE HYNES. an what about somethin to do

THERESA BLACK. get them to clean the yard

JOE HYNES. we've done that

THERESA BLACK. tell them there's an inspection of the yard as well – get them to do it again

JOE HYNES. inspection – they're not fuckin stupid ya know

THERESA BLACK. it's the only thing i can think of

JOE HYNES. this isn't on

THERESA BLACK. no

JOE HYNES. it's not – somethin has to be sorted out

THERESA BLACK. a know – it's not up to me but i'm tryin – you can see that can't ya – go an tell them about the inspection

JOE HYNES. when will ya know the full story

THERESA BLACK. you'll know when i know

10

The pub. BOBBIE *and* SHANKS *are at the bar.* HELEN *is serving them.*

SHANKS O'NEILL. first of the day

BOBBIE TORBETT. weren't ya garglin in the house

SHANKS O'NEILL. first a the day in here

BOBBIE TORBETT. square the woman up there

SHANKS O'NEILL. oh aye – alright now – a pint in front a ya – tosspot was it

BOBBIE TORBETT. square her up

Shanks pays for the drinks.

HELEN WOODS. was there many at it

SHANKS O'NEILL. not as big a crowd as you'd like if ya were dead yerself

BOBBIE TORBETT. there's been bigger alright – not surprisin miserable fucker he was

HELEN WOODS. did the mention about comin back here

BOBBIE TORBETT. you'll not be rushed off yer feet

SHANKS O'NEILL. see the sons weren't talkin still

BOBBIE TORBETT. no

SHANKS O'NEILL. you'd think with a funeral an that

HELEN WOODS. maybe sort out some sandwiches for them

SHANKS O'NEILL. aye helen make a few sandwiches – forgot to eat yesterday

BOBBIE TORBETT. forgot fuck all – told ya to go home an eat – wouldn't hear of it – food's only for wankers apparently

SHANKS O'NEILL. when i've a drink in me a go a bit deaf in both my ears

BOBBIE TORBETT. not too deaf when yer asked what ya want to gargle

SHANKS O'NEILL. it's only certain words a can't hear

HELEN WOODS. home

SHANKS O'NEILL. what

HELEN WOODS. i'll go in here an see if there's anythin for sandwiches just in case

SHANKS O'NEILL. smoked salmon be nice

HELEN WOODS. aye – any punters come in give us a shout

BOBBIE TORBETT. will do

HELEN *exits*.

nice wee girl that

SHANKS O'NEILL. too young for you – do me though

BOBBIE TORBETT. i'm just sayin

SHANKS O'NEILL. she does a line with yer man

BOBBIE TORBETT. who

SHANKS O'NEILL. guy works at the plant – married like – don't know his name – in here now an again – always on the phone

BOBBIE TORBETT. him

SHANKS O'NEILL. aye him

BOBBIE TORBETT. fuck yer woman callin round last night – she starts thinkin like that she'll end up callin round everytime the two a them give each other a dirty look

SHANKS O'NEILL. she'll not

BOP TORBETT. not be back today anyway

SHANKS O'NEILL. no

BOBBIE TORBETT. not know where we are – don't want her spoilin a good drink

SHANKS O'NEILL. no – what do ya call masters' secretary

BOBBIE TORBETT. theresa – she's a right woman now

SHANKS O'NEILL. she was there

BOBBIE TORBETT. saw her – always liked her – losin the son didn't do her any favours

SHANKS O'NEILL. ya should've been over at her sayin about the wee lad an the job – she'd be the one to talk to

BOBBIE TORBETT. say nothin about the meat plant when he's about

SHANKS O'NEILL. ya not want him workin

BOBBIE TORBETT. a don't want him workin in that fuckin kip

SHANKS O'NEILL. carryin the meat never did me any harm

BOBBIE TORBETT. carryin what meat – not a day's work in ya

SHANKS O'NEILL. i worked there with the best a them a did

BOBBIE TORBETT. aye

SHANKS O'NEILL. no aye about it

BOBBIE TORBETT. aye – you just keep thinkin that – he's not endin up like i did – back wrecked an not even a fuckin thank you for it – so say fuck all

SHANKS O'NEILL. aye

BOBBIE TORBETT. i'm tellin ya

SHANKS O'NEILL. a heard – i'm not fuckin deaf

BOBBIE TORBETT. right

Silence. HELEN *enters.*

HELEN WOODS. no smoked salmon – a bit a ham an chicken – it'll have to do

BOBBIE TORBETT. do them rightly

HELEN WOODS. ya like to have somethin at these things – doesn't look good if there's nothin

PAUL *enters.*

SHANKS O'NEILL. here we go

BOBBIE TORBETT. what do ya call him

SHANKS O'NEILL. harry

BOBBIE TORBETT. sure

SHANKS O'NEILL. aye

BOBBIE TORBETT. harry sorry for yer troubles

PAUL FOGGARTY. paul – my name's paul – i've a brother harry

BOBBIE TORBETT. paul – of course – sorry for yer troubles anyway

SHANKS O'NEILL. aye paul sorry for yer troubles an that

PAUL FOGGARTY. aye bad day – you want a pint or are you alright

SHANKS O'NEILL. go another pint

BOBBIE TORBETT. we'll have a drink for yer da – great man he was – knew him well

PAUL FOGGARTY (*to* HELEN). three pints there

HELEN WOODS. a wasn't sure whether to put some sandwiches out

PAUL FOGGARTY. ya want a few sandwiches

SHANKS O'NEILL. a couple a sandwiches do rightly paul

BOBBIE TORBETT. aye

PAUL FOGGARTY. do enough for the three a us – more if ya want some yerself

HELEN WOODS. i'll get ya the pints then i'll sort the sandwiches out

After getting the drinks HELEN *exits*.

PAUL FOGGARTY (*to* BOBBIE). ya worked with my da then

BOBBIE TORBETT. a did – worked with him for a right few years

SHANKS O'NEILL. a worked with him myself

BOBBIE TORBETT. good worker he was yer da – always said that about him – good worker

PAUL FOGGARTY. ya think there'd a been more at the funeral

BOBBIE TORBETT. people's funny fuckers about funerals – makes them think about dyin – the don't like that

PAUL FOGGARTY. a thought the abattoir might a closed though

SHANKS O'NEILL. money hungry whores the are paul

PAUL FOGGARTY. there was a few there a didn't know – but then a man has a life of his own whether he's yer da or not

BOBBIE TORBETT. that's right – only a knew them in my own right there was ones at my da's funeral a wouldn't've known he knew

SHANKS O'NEILL. aye that's right

PAUL FOGGARTY. we'll have a drink to him anyway (*All lift pints*.) to big dan god rest him

SHANKS O'NEILL. big dan

BOBBIE TORBETT. big dan

PAUL FOGGARTY. i'll nip out here an see – in case any others are about ya know

PAUL *exits*.

BOBBIE TORBETT. big dan – who the fuck is big dan

SHANKS O'NEILL. what ya mean who the fuck is he – his da – the guy the just fired into the ground

BOBBIE TORBETT. big dan's not his fuckin name

SHANKS O'NEILL. yer tellin me he got his own da's name wrong

BOBBIE TORBETT. i don't know what the fuck he did

SHANKS O'NEILL. he'd know his own da's name bobbie for fuck's sake

BOBBIE TORBETT. no big dan – man a worked with was called john – ya not know him

SHANKS O'NEILL. not really no – maybe the guy ya worked with wasn't him

BOBBIE TORBETT. the man a worked with wasn't him – how the fuck can it not be him – john foggarty ya called the man – that's his son harry

SHANKS O'NEILL. paul

BOBBIE TORBETT. aye whatever – paul – harry – that's his son anyway – an i'll tell ya another thing – he was the size of a fuckin sixpence – nothing big about him

SHANKS O'NEILL. maybe it was his brother or somethin

BOBBIE TORBETT. how can the guy a worked with be the brother of the guy a worked with – you lost yer fuckin mind

SHANKS O'NEILL. ya know what a mean – ask him

BOBBIE TORBETT. ask him – i've just been to the guy's da's funeral an a told him a worked with his da for years – an then i'm goin to say by the way what's yer da's name – fuckin wise up

PAUL *enters*.

SHANKS O'NEILL. i'll ask him

PAUL FOGGARTY. nah – doesn't look like anyone else comin

SHANKS O'NEILL. paul – yer da

PAUL FOGGARTY. aye

SHANKS O'NEILL. john ya called him

PAUL FOGGARTY. aye

SHANKS O'NEILL. you said god rest big dan

PAUL FOGGARTY. aye right – in the house that's what he liked us callin him – sure he wasn't big either

BOBBIE TORBETT. a knew that – he wasn't a big man at all – the meat he was carryin was bigger

PAUL FOGGARTY. big dan god rest him

SHANKS O'NEILL. aye – saw yer brother at the funeral

PAUL FOGGARTY. fucker

SHANKS O'NEILL. you an him not get on no

PAUL FOGGARTY. haven't spoken this – must be fifteen years – fuckin useless bastard he is

SHANKS O'NEILL. he'll hardly be weighing in then

PAUL FOGGARTY. a wouldn't want him near me – sure the three of us is enough

BOBBIE TORBETT. three's plenty

PAUL FOGGARTY. knock that into ya we'll have another

SHANKS O'NEILL. that's the game

11

The street. BOP *and* MAGGIE. *She has swimming gear with her.*

MAGGIE LYTTLE. yer just goin to stand here all day

BOP TORBETT. don't know

MAGGIE LYTTLE. a thought ya wanted to go with me

BOP TORBETT. a don't feel like it

MAGGIE LYTTLE. i'm not goin on my own

BOP TORBETT. get cooper to go

MAGGIE LYTTLE. i didn't ask cooper

BOP TORBETT. we'll go some other day

MAGGIE LYTTLE. are ya goin or not

BOP TORBETT. no

MAGGIE LYTTLE. right

They stand in silence. COOPER *and* SWIZ *enter.* COOPER *has a large plastic bag of sweets.*

COOPER JONES. the bop fella – and the maggie girl – who

wants some sweeties – sweeties for the children – all types
a sweeties

BOP TORBETT. they from last night

COOPER JONES. last night was last night today is today

SWIZ MURDOCK. cooper an swiz – the criminals

MAGGIE LYTTLE. nothin more than tea leaves

SWIZ MURDOCK. masterminds of the criminal world

COOPER JONES. look – born with no fingerprints – maggie
baby want some sweets

MAGGIE LYTTLE. give us a bar a chocolate

COOPER JONES. the bop fella sweeties

BOP TORBETT. nah a just put one out

COOPER JONES. no other takers – fuck that then (*Throws
bag away.*)

BOP TORBETT (*to* SWIZ). ya not at work today

SWIZ MURDOCK. fuck work

COOPER JONES. the swizman says fuck work

SWIZ MURDOCK. not for us – too good lookin for that place
– aren't a too good lookin for that place maggie

MAGGIE LYTTLE. better lookin cattle there

COOPER JONES. moo – moo

SWIZ MURDOCK. moo – moo

COOPER JONES. the moo people

SWIZ MURDOCK. where'd ya go last night bop

BOP TORBETT. nowhere

COOPER JONES. moo – moo maggie – go moo

MAGGIE LYTTLE. take off ya header

COOPER JONES. go on

MAGGIE LYTTLE. moo – fucking – moo

SWIZ MURDOCK. lapped the show

MAGGIE LYTTLE. more sense he has

COOPER JONES. the bop fella has more sense – have i no sense dearest

MAGGIE LYTTLE. yer just a big lig

COOPER JONES. i'm deeply hurt – the woman of my dreams thinks i'm a big lig – an me who just give her chocolate

SWIZ MURDOCK. a don't like it when he runs off

BOP TORBETT. a didn't run off

COOPER JONES. the swiz fella – the man who says fuck work

SWIZ MURDOCK. fuck work

COOPER JONES. bop isn't into the hurdy gurdy – stop gettin on his case

SWIZ MURDOCK. lapped the show

COOPER JONES. leave him

SWIZ MURDOCK. moo

COOPER JONES (*to* MAGGIE). what's in the bag – ya goin somewhere

MAGGIE LYTTLE. i'm not standin here all day

COOPER JONES. waste yer talents standin here all day – a don't think so

MAGGIE LYTTLE. a was goin to go swimmin

COOPER JONES. the swimmers – the piss in the water there

MAGGIE LYTTLE. the river up by the park

COOPER JONES. ya want me to go – i'll go

MAGGIE LYTTLE. ya want to go swimmin

COOPER JONES. in school i used to swim the shit out a the rest a them

SWIZ MURDOCK. moo

MAGGIE LYTTLE. you've no gear with ya

COOPER JONES. that meant to matter – we'll go now – the water's callin me and when the river calls the trunks get wet

SWIZ MURDOCK. ya be about later sort some gear out

COOPER JONES. oh aye – we'll be back later

MAGGIE LYTTLE. unless ya plan livin there

COOPER JONES. moo

SWIZ MURDOCK. moo

> COOPER *and* MAGGIE *exit*. BOP *and* SWIZ *stand in silence*.

> just me an you bop – ya goin anywhere

BOP TORBETT. nah – you

SWIZ MURDOCK. aye – last night the druggie – my brother wants me to stand outside his flat – nothin major just wants to know the fucker's movements – ya wanna go – be better than standin here

BOP TORBETT. the guy's a screwball

SWIZ MURDOCK. just standin lookin – don't be lappin the show again bop

BOP TORBETT. i'm not

SWIZ MURDOCK. get a few fabulets out of it do us for tonight – mon

BOP TORBETT. aye alright

12

The flat. ROBBIE *is dressed in a suit. He is getting ready to go out*. CONNIE *is restless. She is still at the window*.

CONNIE DEAN. why can't a go with ya

ROBBIE MULLIN. yer not goin you'll get in the way

CONNIE DEAN. i'm sick a stayin here on my own

ROBBIE MULLIN. i'm not takin all the gear and there's
readies in the bedroom as well – that's why yer stayin –
stop fuckin hasslin me – not like yer asked to do much is it

CONNIE DEAN. what happens if someone comes

ROBBIE MULLIN. the won't

CONNIE DEAN. i'll be on my own – ya shouldn't leave me
on my own robbie

ROBBIE MULLIN. a don't want the place empty – that money
is all we've got – place is like a fuckin fortress anyway
what ya worried about

CONNIE DEAN. i'm just worried

ROBBIE MULLIN. don't be treatin me like one of those
fuckin half wits works down in that meat place – the think
it's all right that they get a pile of grief from whatever
scrubber they've shacked up with before the leave for work
– that's not me an don't ever fuckin think that it's gonna be
me – ya got that

CONNIE DEAN. i'm only sayin

ROBBIE MULLIN. you goin out with me changes the
situation – if the situation changes that might make it
difficult to get rid a things – what would happen then – tell
me

CONNIE DEAN. a don't know

ROBBIE MULLIN. no ya don't fuckin know – the money in
there not goin to do us long – have to fuckin slum it – i'm
not doin that – we need more money – that's the only thing
these people's interested in – the colour of yer readies – do
all the talkin ya want but unless ya have the money to back
it up you'll be treated like a joke – doesn't matter what
deals or whatever you've pulled off before – means nothing
– an that's the right way to do it too

CONNIE DEAN. ya goin now

ROBBIE MULLIN. soon

CONNIE DEAN. i need somethin before ya go

ROBBIE MULLIN. there's odds an ends in that drawer – don't be gettin all fucked up

CONNIE DEAN. a don't get all fucked up

ROBBIE MULLIN. a mean it – ya need yer head about ya

CONNIE DEAN. in the drawer over there

ROBBIE MULLIN. didn't a just say

CONNIE DEAN. ya goin to bring back some food

ROBBIE MULLIN. like what

CONNIE DEAN. somethin nice

ROBBIE MULLIN. somethin nice – aye – pack a few suitcases while i'm out

CONNIE DEAN. a don't know what to take

ROBBIE MULLIN. whatever the fuck we need

CONNIE DEAN. there's two wee lads across the street – just standin there the are

ROBBIE MULLIN (*looks*). don't know them – you know them

CONNIE DEAN. a don't go anywhere – if you don't know them i don't know them

ROBBIE MULLIN. just kids – have fuck all to do but hang around – wouldn't worry about it – just kids – i'll phone later right

CONNIE DEAN. right

ROBBIE MULLIN. take it easy – member what a said

CONNIE DEAN. you'll phone me

ROBBIE MULLIN. get the cases packed – yer the only person i can trust – remember that

He kisses her then lifts his bag and exits. CONNIE *goes straight to the drawer.*

13

The pub. HELEN is behind the bar. There are two plates of half eaten sandwiches on the counter. BOBBIE, SHANKS and PAUL are standing at the bar. BOBBIE is in the middle of telling a joke.

BOBBIE TORBETT. i've never seen a horse that fast in my life – but tell me this – why'd it run into the oaktree – yer man says – a don't know – it just doesn't give a fuck

Laughter except SHANKS.

SHANKS O'NEILL. i don't get that

BOBBIE TORBETT. it just doesn't give a fuck

SHANKS O'NEILL. an what

BOBBIE TORBETT. doesn't matter

SHANKS O'NEILL. it's not funny

BOBBIE TORBETT. aye

HARRY FOGGARTY *enters. He stands at the other end of the bar.*

HARRY FOGGARTY (*to* HELEN). a pint please (*Silence.*) yous boys at the funeral

BOBBIE TORBETT. aye – knew yer da well

HARRY FOGGARTY. you want a pint

SHANKS O'NEILL. do rightly

HARRY FOGGARTY (*to* HELEN). another three pints

PAUL FOGGARTY (*to* HELEN). i don't want one

HARRY FOGGARTY. take one

PAUL FOGGARTY (*to* HELEN). a don't want one

HARRY FOGGARTY. not such a big crowd there

BOBBIE TORBETT. there's ones that has nobody at them

HARRY FOGGARTY. except the poor bugger that's dead

BOBBIE TORBETT. funerals wouldn't be the same without them

HARRY FOGGARTY. ya knew my da then

BOBBIE TORBETT. aye – a worked with him – carryin the meat

HARRY FOGGARTY. hard ole number that

BOBBIE TORBETT. it can be

PAUL FOGGARTY. yer not wanted here

HARRY FOGGARTY. i'm havin a pint

PAUL FOGGARTY. have it some place else

HELEN *sets drinks up.*

HELEN WOODS. there's sandwiches there – a wasn't sure how many – ya want me to make more

PAUL FOGGARTY. he's not stayin

HARRY FOGGARTY. it's alright luv a drink'll do me (*Raises glass.*) my da

BOBBIE TORBETT. big dan god rest him

SHANKS O'NEILL. to big dan god rest him

HARRY FOGGARTY. big dan – a forgot about that (*To* PAUL.) not raisin your glass

PAUL FOGGARTY. not with you ya fuckin ponce

HARRY FOGGARTY. that it – you goin to sort me out are ya – big lad – don't be makin a fool a yerself in front a these people

PAUL *lunges.* BOBBIE *holds him back.*

PAUL FOGGARTY. get out to fuck – frightened a you – fuck off

HARRY FOGGARTY. let him go

PAUL FOGGARTY. fuckin ponce

BOBBIE TORBETT. it's yer da's funeral lads

PAUL FOGGARTY. he doesn't give a fuck whose funeral it is

HARRY FOGGARTY. a give as much of a fuck as you do

PAUL FOGGARTY. ponce

HARRY FOGGARTY. i'm warnin ya

PAUL FOGGARTY. don't fuckin warn anybody

BOBBIE TORBETT. give it a break here

HELEN WOODS. i don't care whose funeral it was any
trouble an ya have to go

BOBBIE TORBETT. there'll be no trouble

HELEN WOODS. take yer drink an eat yer sandwiches

BOBBIE TORBETT. that's right eat the sandwiches

Everything is settled.

HARRY FOGGARTY. we need to talk

BOBBIE TORBETT. that's a start

HARRY FOGGARTY. i've a letter here

PAUL FOGGARTY. want me to read it to ya

HARRY FOGGARTY. some man at the funeral give it to me –
a didn't know him – it's from my da

PAUL FOGGARTY. what he give it to you for

HARRY FOGGARTY. don't know – my da wanted us to read
it together he said

PAUL FOGGARTY. that's not goin to happen

HARRY FOGGARTY. it's what my da wanted – i'm goin to
sit down over there at that table – you want to sit down with
me fine if ya don't it's up to you.

HARRY sits at the table.

BOBBIE TORBETT. yer better goin over

SHANKS O'NEILL. that's right

BOBBIE TORBETT. big dan – the man's dead an that's what
he wanted – yer always better of doin what dead people
want – bad vibes from the grave isn't good

PAUL *sits at the table*.

HARRY FOGGARTY. i'm not happy about this either

PAUL FOGGARTY. just open the letter harry an read it

HARRY FOGGARTY (*opening letter*). a bigger crowd
would've been better

PAUL FOGGARTY. people's other things to do

HARRY FOGGARTY. aye

PAUL FOGGARTY. what's it say

HARRY FOGGARTY. read it yerself

PAUL FOGGARTY. settle yer differences – that's it – a note
that says settle yer differences

HARRY FOGGARTY. there's another sheet a paper here

PAUL FOGGARTY. what is it

HARRY FOGGARTY. his own writing it's in – a list

PAUL FOGGARTY. a list a what

HARRY FOGGARTY. jesus – a list of everything he owned –
look at that – man sat down and wrote everything out that
he owned – doesn't look like much does it

PAUL FOGGARTY. no – fuck this – we to divide this up then
aye

HARRY FOGGARTY. ya want to go somewhere else an do
this

PAUL FOGGARTY. where

SHARON *arrives with her suitcase and sets it down beside*
BOBBIE *and* SHANKS.

ACT TWO

The middle of the day.

1

The shop. ROBBIE *and* SAMMY *are in mid conversation.*
BETTY *is checking a list of goods that have been delivered.*

SAMMY LENNON. like freezer bags ya mean

ROBBIE MULLIN. they'd be too big

SAMMY LENNON. too big – next down from that would be
sandwich bags – (*To* BETTY.) did the deliver any sandwich
bags

BETTY LENNON. no – but he has to come back this
afternoon

ROBBIE MULLIN. i'd really need them now

SAMMY LENNON. might be some over in the corner there

BETTY LENNON. that's that checked off – whatever comes
in this afternoon sammy you've to check off – you forgot
the last time

SAMMY LENNON. i didn't forget – tryin to pull a flanker on
me he was

BETTY LENNON. just check it off sammy

SAMMY LENNON. ya see sandwich bags about here

BETTY LENNON. can't remember seein them – i've done my
list so i'm away to organise my taxi

SAMMY LENNON. aye you do that

BETTY *exits.*

things are still in a bit of a mess here – i'd a break in last
night – everythin messed up – not sure where everythin is

ROBBIE MULLIN. kids was it

SAMMY LENNON. aye bloody kids – oven bags – what would they be – no – same size as the freezer bags

ROBBIE MULLIN. peelers are never about when ya need them

SAMMY LENNON. damn the fear of it – didn't phone them – the only thing a have here are kids' party bags – that hardly be of any use to ya

ROBBIE MULLIN. let's have a look at them

SAMMY LENNON. there's twenty in that

ROBBIE MULLIN. twenty's plenty – right size – kids' party bags – aye they'll do – security ya need

SAMMY LENNON. a was thinkin that – an awful price a hear

ROBBIE MULLIN. i've a card here – always worth yer while keepin these things – ring them

SAMMY LENNON. a will – although you'd wonder whether it stops them or not – drugged up to the eyeballs nothin stop them

ROBBIE MULLIN. baseball bat is the job

SAMMY LENNON. now yer talkin – i've an ole club up there a was thinkin of goin up to get it

ROBBIE MULLIN. split a few nappers open

SAMMY LENNON. ya wonder what the hell's goin on – wee girl in here this mornin – first thing – drugged up she was – what way is that to be before the world's awake – she looked ill to me – eatin the amount of chocolate she bought make anybody ill – not that i'm complainin about sellin it

ROBBIE MULLIN. chocolate

SAMMY LENNON. aye – must've been for her breakfast

ROBBIE MULLIN. right – what a owe ya for the bags

SAMMY LENNON. give us a pound

BETTY *enters*

BETTY LENNON. every taxi firm booked – nothin for at least half an hour

SAMMY LENNON. ya gonna be late

BETTY LENNON. a don't like rushin

ROBBIE MULLIN. where is it yer goin

SAMMY LENNON. she's headin up to the hospital

ROBBIE MULLIN. i've business up there – i'll give ya a lift

BETTY LENNON. you don't mind

ROBBIE MULLIN. not at all

SAMMY LENNON. i hate her in taxis – read somewhere that it's them that delivers the drugs all over the city – never know what would happen

BETTY LENNON. the can't all be doin that sammy

ROBBIE MULLIN. better safe than sorry – i'll wait for ya outside – parked out the front

ROBBIE *exits*.

SAMMY LENNON. that's a right fella that

BETTY LENNON. you remember about the new order

SAMMY LENNON. yes – don't you be worryin about anythin it's only a check up

BETTY LENNON. stop fussin over me

SAMMY LENNON. ya got everything

BETTY LENNON. i've my bag that's all a need

SAMMY LENNON. not be long anyway

BETTY LENNON. aye

2

The abattoir. THERESA's *office. She is about to make a phone call.* DAVE *enters.*

DAVE BLACK (*to workers below*). aye – ya wouldn't know a day's graft if it spat in yer eye

THERESA BLACK (*puts phone down*). what are you doin here

DAVE BLACK. that's lovely

THERESA BLACK. ya know what a mean

DAVE BLACK. the wouldn't let me on the radio – said the might later but a wasn't goin to hang around for that

THERESA BLACK. i said the wouldn't

DAVE BLACK. a know ya did – how's things goin here – they're givin out down there about hangin around

THERESA BLACK. still waitin to hear word

DAVE BLACK. gettin close to the wire is it

THERESA BLACK. there's been easier days

DAVE BLACK. aye right – a want ya to phone yer brian an get me a lend of his car – i'm goin to drive down to the dig

THERESA BLACK. what for

DAVE BLACK. see if a can get somethin done

THERESA BLACK. yer suspended from drivin

DAVE BLACK. he doesn't know that

THERESA BLACK. still

DAVE BLACK. still nothin – phone him – i'd do it only he'd give me a lot a shit over the phone – ya know what he's like – think he was the only one ever to own a car

THERESA BLACK. i'm not phonin him

DAVE BLACK. the only other way's the bus – phone him

THERESA BLACK. i'm not phonin him

DAVE BLACK. why you doin this to me

THERESA BLACK. i'm not doin anythin

DAVE BLACK. correct – yer not helpin me are ya – a don't understand yer attitude

THERESA BLACK. i'm in the middle a work

DAVE BLACK. since they've started diggin there's been a change

THERESA BLACK. there's no change – i've work to do – i'm under pressure here can you not see that

DAVE BLACK. it's like ya don't want them to dig

THERESA BLACK. don't be bloody stupid

DAVE BLACK. a don't understan that – the have to look theresa – if the don't look the won't find him

THERESA BLACK. go get yer bus

DAVE BLACK. why don't ya come with me – if both of us are there together the case for keepin it all goin would be better – stronger

THERESA BLACK. i'm needed here

DAVE BLACK. what if the ask where ya are

THERESA BLACK. nobody's goin to ask anythin dave

DAVE BLACK. what if the do – say i start shoutin the odds – this is important to us – you have to keep diggin because it's important to us – what if someone says – where's yer wife – where's the mother of this child – sorry but she couldn't make it today – busy at work she tells me – what type of person are they goin to think you are

THERESA BLACK. the type that's kept us goin all these years – the type that gets on with what the have to do in order to keep our lives together – do you know what it's like to have to look an listen to you this last fifteen years – all the time wimperin in my face – like ya were the only person ever felt any pain – yer like an open wound

DAVE BLACK. i'd rather be like that than the way you are

THERESA BLACK. what way would that be – lookin after you ya mean – go to work dave – eat yer food dave – go to

the doctor dave – go to sleep dave – they're goin to stop
diggin an now yer goin to do something – it's too late

DAVE BLACK. least a haven't given up – if our child was to
walk through that door right now a be ashamed for ya – you
couldn't look him straight in the eye

THERESA BLACK. get out

DAVE BLACK. oh i'm goin all right – i'm goin to where you
should be only ya haven't the balls to go – you couldn't
look him in the eye because you've stopped carin

THERESA BLACK. get out

DAVE BLACK. another thing – tell yer brother to stick his car
up his fuckin hole

*DAVE exits. THERESA composes herself then lifts the
phone.*

3

*The river. MAGGIE and COOPER are drying off after a swim.
FRANK COIN is some distance away sitting on a park bench.*

MAGGIE LYTTLE. what was it – oh aye – i used to swim the
shit out a them when a was at school – spoof

COOPER JONES. a did – haven't been in the water for a
while that's all (*Poses.*) what do ya think a that – there's
wankers pays a fortune to be like that – with me it's just
natural

MAGGIE LYTTLE. big girlie spoof

COOPER JONES. didn't a save you from drownin there

MAGGIE LYTTLE. gropin me under the water isn't savin me
from drownin

COOPER JONES. it keeps yer head up above the water

They lie on the grass.

MAGGIE LYTTLE. i think a could live here

COOPER JONES. fuck all but fields

MAGGIE LYTTLE. the city's fuck all but streets

COOPER JONES. streets are good fields are fucked – country people are a bit iffy

MAGGIE LYTTLE. iffy what way

COOPER JONES. always on about sheep – sheep an cows – like those balloons down at the plant – ask swiz about them

MAGGIE LYTTLE. swiz is a dick

COOPER JONES. ya not like swiz no

MAGGIE LYTTLE. he's a dick

COOPER JONES. he's alright

MAGGIE LYTTLE. he's too nasty – see it in his face sometimes

COOPER JONES. he is nasty – but then all his ones are nasty bastards – got a job

MAGGIE LYTTLE. thought you were a fuck work type a guy

COOPER JONES. a do think like that but this job's sound

MAGGIE LYTTLE. head commando of the head commandoes

COOPER JONES. i'd make a fucking fine commando let me tell ya

MAGGIE LYTTLE. on dry land

COOPER JONES. doin the door at the club

MAGGIE LYTTLE. did ya not say a job

COOPER JONES. a get money – an none a that other sandwiches for lunch shit

MAGGIE LYTTLE. a job job

COOPER JONES. a job job is a no no – be alright – the guy's that doin it is movin on soon to something else

MAGGIE LYTTLE. rocket science

COOPER JONES. the very thing – he deals with rockets already doesn't he – i'll let ya in for nothin

MAGGIE LYTTLE. that meant to be a bonus is it

COOPER JONES. see the guy on the door that's my fella –
jesus you're one lucky duck

MAGGIE LYTTLE. yer so full a shit

COOPER JONES. darling

MAGGIE LYTTLE. yer so full a shit darling

COOPER JONES. tell me this

MAGGIE LYTTLE. this is goin to be somethin deep isn't it –
yer not normally into the deep but yer goin to surprise me

COOPER JONES. what might be deep for me mightn't be for
you

MAGGIE LYTTLE. a bet ya a know what yer goin to say

COOPER JONES. what

MAGGIE LYTTLE. any chance of a blowjob

COOPER JONES. a wasn't goin to say that but we're both
thinkin along the right lines (*He rolls over on top of her.*)
the heat makes me horny does it not you

MAGGIE LYTTLE. it does

COOPER JONES (*hand between her legs*). ya want to hear
what my plan is

MAGGIE LYTTLE. in front a that ole lad over there

COOPER JONES. fuck him – (*Shouts.*) go away home ya
lonely ole fucker

They kiss.

4

The flat and the street outside. CONNIE *has the music on. She
is packing, dancing, drinking and trying on tops.* BOP *and*
SWIZ *are in the street watching the flat.*

SWIZ MURDOCK. the inside a that flat be the business

BOP TORBETT. ya reckon

SWIZ MURDOCK. that's where the spondi is – that's the work ya want to be at – fuck that chasin cattle business

BOP TORBETT. the not bothered about ya not weighin in today

SWIZ MURDOCK. don't care

BOP TORBETT. not sack ya

SWIZ MURDOCK. sack away all the like – get a few quid for doin this – some fabulets on top a that – better off

BOP TORBETT. i'm gettin my da to put a word in for me

SWIZ MURDOCK. the sack me ya can have my lunchbox – ya think he has a jacuzzi – bet ya the fucker has a jacuzzi – bet ya he gives her one in it – yer woman – his girl – i wouldn't be too long wangin one into her – all that water an bubbles up round yer jamroll – maybe get cramps – cooper maybe has a touch of the cramps now – what do ya reckon bop – cooper wangin away

BOP TORBETT. nothin to do with me

SWIZ MURDOCK. think the rest of us has no eyes – the lovely maggie – i'd give her one – although cooper catch ya yer fucked – it's all about not gettin caught – a gave my brother's girl one – he's not with her now – don't be sayin just in case it gets back to him – a don't think he liked her – just right the dirty bitch

CONNIE *appears at the window. She has no top on.*

fuck look at that – look at yer woman – (*Shouts up.*) show us yer diddies big girl

CONNIE *laughs and flashes her breasts.*

that's it ya girl ye – get the lot off dear – look at the diddies on her

CONNIE *moves away from the window.*

she's in there on her own – bored off her napper – fuckin meat plant aye

CONNIE *is back at the window. She has a top on.*

there she's back again – get them out for the boys dear

CONNIE *throws a bunch of keys out on to the street.* SWIZ *picks them up.* CONNIE *moves away from the window.*

we're in young man we're in

5

The hospital. BETTY *is sitting on her own.* MAEVE *enters.*

MAEVE HYNES. ya made it then – the taxi driver didn't steal ya for the slave trade

BETTY LENNON. sammy worries too much – i got lost walkin about this place – sittin here havin a rest

MAEVE HYNES. it's a wonder anyone can find their way around here

BETTY LENNON. it is a bit confusin

MAEVE HYNES. the whole place is badly designed – look where we are sittin outside the cancer an two steps away is the labour – it's a bit insensitive

BETTY LENNON. a suppose it is

MAEVE HYNES. women goin in there to have babies beside a ward where they're all dyin – coughin an splutterin everywhere

BETTY LENNON. not everyone in there is dyin i'm sure

MAEVE HYNES. once yer in there there's not much hope – a don't blame those poor souls a blame the hospital – could've planned it better

BETTY LENNON. yer cousin isn't it – has she had the baby yet

MAEVE HYNES. not yet – should be soon though

BETTY LENNON. just nipped out for a breather

MAEVE HYNES. the midwife asked me to leave – she said a was too nervous an a was makin the mother nervous – i've to calm down

BETTY LENNON. i'm sure they'll let ya back in

MAEVE HYNES. she needs a face she knows to hold her hand

BETTY LENNON. people need support at times like this

MAEVE HYNES. it isn't easy in there holdin yer nerve

BETTY LENNON. no i'd say not

MAEVE HYNES. the poor girl's hooked up to everything – it makes ya think what can go wrong

BETTY LENNON. she's in the best place

MAEVE HYNES. that's true – it's just ya worry don't ya

BETTY LENNON. some worry an some don't – sammy worries about everythin under the sun – ends up ya can't tell him anythin he makes a fuss – things you should be tellin him

MAEVE HYNES. some a the women in there – you'd worry more about the wee babies then ya would anythin else – what type a life's out there for them

BETTY LENNON. most seem to get through it

MAEVE HYNES. but to see them – wee girls – fegs in their mouths – the baby in the cot an they're up at the smokin room puffin away – not interested in holdin the children – there's one in there – face covered in tattoos an the hair dyed off herself – wouldn't hold the baby – gets the nurse to look after him – the shouts of her – what type a life is that wee child gonna have – his mother won't even hold him – i'd half a mind to lift the child up an give it a nurse myself

BETTY LENNON. you'd need to be careful about that – the mother wouldn't thank ya for it

MAEVE HYNES. i've half a mind to do it none the less – they should be taken off them an given to people that's goin to care for them – that's the worry isn't it – that bad things are goin to happen to those wee children – bloody disgrace

BETTY LENNON. don't be getting all upset

MAEVE HYNES. i can't help it – it just makes me feel crazy

BETTY LENNON. you're to go back in there remember

MAEVE HYNES. the shouldn't have children – here's me rantin on an a haven't asked ya about yer check up

BETTY LENNON. it's nothing – everything's alright

MAEVE HYNES. were ya havin tests taken or were the given ya the results of ones the had taken – i was in here a few months back – needle after needle – x rays – more needles – a sample of this a sample of that – treated like a bloody piece of meat ya are – the nurse was lovely though – the doctor a had no time for but the nurse was lovely – the job the have to do too – can ya picture what it's like in that ward for them – dyin or not dyin lookin after those poor souls must be a messy business (BETTY *stands to leave*.)

BETTY LENNON. i'd better go

MAEVE HYNES. once i've got the better of my nerves i'll head back in – she needs me to look after her doesn't she

6

The abattoir. THERESA *sits behind her desk in her office.*

THERESA BLACK (*speaking on the intercom*). would joe hynes come to the office please – joe hynes to the office

JOE *enters.*

JOE HYNES. get some exercise up and down those stairs today – by the way one a the wee lads down in the bonin yard – stupid wee bastard he is – messin about with the knives – he's opened his hand up – first aid box was no good so he's on his way to the hospital – he hardly be back so i'll collect his wages for him

THERESA BLACK. did ya write it all down in the accident book

JOE HYNES. aye – a told him all about the claim forms an that

THERESA BLACK. thought it was his fault

JOE HYNES. his fault or not he'll be off work won't he – he'll need a few quid

THERESA BLACK. a was talkin to masters – it's not as straightforward as he thought it was

JOE HYNES. it couldn't be straightforward – that would only get the job done

THERESA BLACK. the deal he's workin on isn't completed – the guy who owns the processin factory is still waitin on a better price so he won't sign

JOE HYNES. we're all fucked then

THERESA BLACK. listen a minute – i want to get one thing clear first – i'm not meant to be tellin ya this

JOE HYNES. why ya tellin me then

THERESA BLACK. because a think it's the right thing to do – it has to be up to you

JOE HYNES. i don't want things left up to me

THERESA BLACK. he's managed to organise something with the bank – they've agreed to give him money before the end of the day but the won't give him all he needs – either he pays for the container at the dock or covers the wages

JOE HYNES. he has to cover the wages – there's no question about that

THERESA BLACK. right – if the container isn't unloaded today it has to go back – he'd still get charged under a time penalty though – if he pays for the container with money he hasn't got he'll have to incorporate that cost into the deal he's workin on at the moment – that along with the euro will put him over his margins – he could lose the whole lot – with nothin comin in that means there's goin to have to be lay offs

JOE HYNES. what are ya tellin me then

THERESA BLACK. i just said joe

JOE HYNES. the deal – what's the deal

THERESA BLACK. unload the container which at least means he has something to sell

JOE HYNES. he hasn't bought it yet

THERESA BLACK. he can sell it before he buys it

JOE HYNES. fuck

THERESA BLACK. the wages would be covered but probably not today

JOE HYNES. yer askin me to tell them to work – then tell them they're not gettin paid

THERESA BLACK. better that than lay offs

JOE HYNES. the container doesn't matter does it – it's not long term

THERESA BLACK. no it's only a way of keepin things tickin over for a few days while something else can be sorted out – it's the other deal that's important

JOE HYNES. if he doesn't get that

THERESA BLACK. he thinks he is goin to get it – there's just a bit of a waitin game goin on

JOE HYNES. i'm meant to be tellin the union all this ya know

THERESA BLACK. what good's that to any one

JOE HYNES. the bottom line is i've to go down an tell them to unload a container an then wait an hope the get paid – who's goin to do that

THERESA BLACK. don't tell them

JOE HYNES. don't tell them what

THERESA BLACK. don't tell them the mightn't be gettin their money at the end of the day

JOE HYNES. you've put me in a position here

THERESA BLACK. unload the container – in the long term it's the best thing to do – but it's yer decision

HELEN *is behind the bar in the pub. She makes a phone call on her mobile.* JOE's *mobile rings.* HELEN *walks into the scene.*

JOE HYNES. sorry about this

HELEN WOODS. i'm bored joe – surrounded by monkeys here – come over an see me

JOE HYNES. i'm talkin to somebody here

HELEN WOODS. are ya talkin about meat joe – tell me what yer goin to do with yer meat joe

JOE HYNES. i'm sure something can be sorted out

HELEN WOODS. i'm hungry joe – i'm goin to eat all yer meat – juicy pink meat

JOE HYNES. that sounds interestin

HELEN WOODS. big joe the meat man – (*Laughs.*) i'm bored joe – come on over – i've a present for ya

JOE HYNES. as well as the meat thing

HELEN WOODS. if yer not here ya won't know

JOE HYNES. sometime later

HELEN WOODS. i'll be waitin meatman

HELEN *exits.*

JOE HYNES. mobile phones – they're a curse – the union give me that one – jesus that's a joke

THERESA BLACK. what are ya goin to do

JOE HYNES. take a meat cleaver to masters that's what

THERESA BLACK. joe – what

JOE HYNES. i'll get them to unload the container – drag it out a bit – not mention anythin about the wages – if nothin comes through by the end a the day there'll be a fuckin riot

THERESA BLACK. i'll chase him all afternoon

JOE HYNES. this container comin from the dock now

THERESA BLACK. not just yet

JOE HYNES. ah come on theresa

THERESA BLACK. he's to find a bank to sign a form – he's drivin round lookin for one right now

JOE HYNES. god bless him

7

The pub. HELEN *is behind the bar.* PAUL *and* HARRY *are standing.* BOBBIE, SHANKS *and* SHARON *are at their table.* HARRY *addresses everyone.*

HARRY FOGGARTY. listen to this a minute

SHANKS O'NEILL. speech speech

BOBBIE TORBETT. listen to the man

HARRY FOGGARTY. there's a couple of items on the list we can't agree on – both of us want this sorted out – so – we'll tell you what the are and why each of us wants them – then ya vote on it

SHANKS O'NEILL. welt away – what's first up

BOBBIE TORBETT. houl yer whist there – goin to a funeral is one thing – big dan god rest him – gettin involved between families an that is another

HARRY FOGGARTY. you'd be doin us a favour

SHARON LAWTHER. do what dead warriors do – burn the lot

SHANKS O'NEILL. whoof – except the stuff ya can sell

BOBBIE TORBETT. we're bein asked to do somethin here – whatever way it goes that's the law a the land

HARRY FOGGARTY. aye (*To* HELEN.) this includes you by the way dear – that alright

HELEN WOODS. i'm not doin anythin else at the moment

HARRY FOGGARTY. the first thing is my da's suit

PAUL FOGGARTY. only suit he had

SHARON LAWTHER. is it a good suit – a good suit is the makings of half a man

HARRY FOGGARTY. yer only suit is yer good suit – i want to keep it to wear it – right – you go

PAUL FOGGARTY. i think it should go to charity – let somebody who needs it get the use of it

SHANKS O'NEILL. i'll take it

HARRY FOGGARTY. wearin yer dead da's suit is passin something on

SHARON LAWTHER. that's a nice suit you've on ya

PAUL FOGGARTY. yer right he doesn't need another one

SHANKS O'NEILL. give it to me

BOBBIE TORBETT. i've a question here – is the suit not too small for ya – big dan wasn't that size

HARRY FOGGARTY. the can be altered can't the

BOBBIE TORBETT. fuck – it would need to be altered a right bit

HARRY FOGGARTY. it's my da's an i want it instead of a complete stranger gettin it

SHANKS O'NEILL. i'm hardly a complete stranger

BOBBIE TORBETT. yer getting nothin

PAUL FOGGARTY. somebody could get the use of it

HARRY FOGGARTY. vote then – whoever thinks i should get the suit put their hands up

SHANKS O'NEILL. it should be a secret ballot

BOBBIE TORBETT. things should always be kept in the family i think

SHARON LAWTHER. whatever bobbie says is right

BOBBIE TORBETT. this is serious

SHARON LAWTHER. i'm agreein with ya

BOBBIE TORBETT. give a reason

SHARON LAWTHER. right – if it doesn't go to him you've no way a knowin who might get it – could be a murderer or anythin

SHANKS O'NEILL. ya would know if i got it

BOBBIE TORBETT. it wouldn't fit you

SHANKS O'NEILL. it doesn't fit him

BOBBIE TORBETT. it makes sense it not fittin him it makes no sense it not fittin you

SHANKS O'NEILL. i vote for charity

Attention turns to HELEN.

HELEN WOODS. my mother died an i still have all her shoes in the house – it wouldn't feel right anyone else havin them

HARRY FOGGARTY. i get the suit – right

SHANKS O'NEILL. what's next up seein a just missed out on a suit

HARRY FOGGARTY. my da had a lot a gardenin equipment

BOBBIE TORBETT. up at them allotments a know that

SHANKS O'NEILL. i've no garden that's me out

HARRY FOGGARTY. i think we should split it – he thinks we should just leave it – do nothin with it

BOBBIE TORBETT. what's the point in that

HARRY FOGGARTY. tell them why ya want that

SHARON LAWTHER. i vote

BOBBIE TORBETT. we're not votin yet

SHARON LAWTHER. hurry up well

PAUL FOGGARTY. the allotment was his pride an joy – any free time he had he spent it up there – the two a us used to go up there with him – that's the only place the three of us spend time together (*To* HARRY.) he told me not to mention this – i'm only sayin it now because of what we're at

HARRY FOGGARTY. he told me not to mention somethin as well

PAUL FOGGARTY. what

HARRY FOGGARTY. you say

PAUL FOGGARTY. alright then fuck it a will – because of this waster my da had to sell the allotment – he came to me an says you had lost money gamblin an ya needed it back so he had to sell the allotment to get it for ya

HARRY FOGGARTY. that's what he told ya

PAUL FOGGARTY. cause that's what happened

HARRY FOGGARTY. he told me you lost money in a game a cards – ya couldn't afford it and he had to sell the allotment to pay it off – that's what he said

PAUL FOGGARTY. what would he do that for

HARRY FOGGARTY. i don't know

BOBBIE TORBETT. the allotment yer talkin about is up round the embankment isn't it

PAUL FOGGARTY. aye

BOBBIE TORBETT. over in the corner beside like a hedge fuckin thing

PAUL FOGGARTY. aye

BOBBIE TORBETT. durin the day i walk up there – yer da sold nothing – every day a was up there i'd see him workin away

PAUL FOGGARTY. big dan

HARRY FOGGARTY. john

BOBBIE TORBETT. yes

HARRY FOGGARTY. up at the allotment

SHARON LAWTHER. bully for big dan – we need another drink here

BOBBIE TORBETT. up there yes (*To* SHARON.) easy on the gargle

SHARON LAWTHER. go buy a drink

SHANKS O'NEILL (*to* SHARON). we'll get that sorted in a minute

PAUL FOGGARTY (*to* BOBBIE). ya sure

BOBBIE TORBETT. i'm not sayin again

PAUL FOGGARTY. a was only sayin

BOBBIE TORBETT. don't fuckin say

HARRY FOGGARTY. don't be gettin all heavy here

BOBBIE TORBETT. what way

HARRY FOGGARTY. don't be slabberin at anyone

BOBBIE TORBETT. that right

SHANKS O'NEILL. bobbie

BOBBIE TORBETT. shut up – a was tellin ya information that was of use to ya – and he's talkin to me like a fuckin child and now yer tellin me i'm slabberin – a don't like that

HARRY FOGGARTY. do ya not

BOBBIE TORBETT. no a don't

SHANKS O'NEILL. i'd leave it lads – different ball game with this man

PAUL FOGGARTY. nobody was sayin that to ya

BOBBIE TORBETT. that's alright then – my mistake

HARRY FOGGARTY. right – i'll get another drink in here

   PAUL *and* HARRY *move to the bar.*

SHARON LAWTHER. only gentleman in the place ya are

BOBBIE TORBETT. a thought ya were goin round to yer sister's

SHARON LAWTHER. not want me here bobbie

SHANKS O'NEILL. yer alright sit there

SHARON LAWTHER. aye i'm alright – goin to the ladies do my face up a bit – mightn't want rid a me then (*Passing* PAUL *and* HARRY *before she exits*.) i vote you to split it up – a spade each

8

The flat. Music is playing. CONNIE *is trying on tops to see which ones she will pack.* SWIZ *and* BOP *are on the sofa smoking a joint.*

CONNIE DEAN. i like this one – wear it if we're goin somewhere special

BOP TORBETT. aye that one that's a good one

SWIZ MURDOCK. the chill out gear

CONNIE DEAN. never get wearin it – no point in takin it

SWIZ MURDOCK. all look the same to me – goin on holiday are ye – topless beach is it – not need any a them

CONNIE DEAN. movin out – on our way – movin out and movin up

SWIZ MURDOCK. today like

CONNIE DEAN. today – the man that looks after me had a bit a trouble at work – you nice boys wouldn't know about that

SWIZ MURDOCK. us nice boys wouldn't – bop sure we wouldn't

CONNIE DEAN. i like it round here

SWIZ MURDOCK. aye round here's the business – me an ya have a boogie – a goin away party

SWIZ *and* CONNIE *dance.*

CONNIE DEAN (*to* BOP). mon dance

BOP TORBETT. my legs are too heavy

SWIZ MURDOCK. that child already has a girl – me on the other hand i've no one

BOP TORBETT. my hands are the big – must have the biggest hands in the world

SWIZ MURDOCK. fuckin massive the are

BOP TORBETT (*laughing*). biggest hands ever made – gloves the size of a ship i'd need for these big fuckers

SWIZ MURDOCK. he's gone

SWIZ *kisses* CONNIE *and starts to pull her skirt up.*

CONNIE DEAN (*stops him*). no no no no no – chill out there a bit

SWIZ MURDOCK. what ya mean – it's party time – no audience – we'll go in there (*Takes her hand.*) mon

CONNIE DEAN. a just want a bit of a laugh

SWIZ MURDOCK. we'll have a laugh in there – mon

CONNIE DEAN. no

SWIZ MURDOCK. what the fuck does that mean no

BOP TORBETT. she says no

SWIZ MURDOCK. fuck up you

BOP TORBETT. what about the hands

SWIZ MURDOCK (*to* CONNIE). i didn't come up here for no

CONNIE DEAN. a don't want everything like that all the time

SWIZ MURDOCK. the window – what the fuck was all that about

CONNIE DEAN. it was funny – a thought that was funny

SWIZ MURDOCK. i like funny – i'm all for funny – a don't like being fuckin messed about though

She kisses him.

CONNIE DEAN. i'm sorry

SWIZ MURDOCK. don't fuckin tease

CONNIE DEAN. never get to talk – just chill out – see what happens

SWIZ MURDOCK. see what happens what

CONNIE DEAN. don't rush in (*She kisses him on the cheek.*) nice girls don't like rushin in

SWIZ MURDOCK. later

CONNIE DEAN. two nice boys

SWIZ MURDOCK. nice boys alright

BOP TORBETT. nice boys with massive fuckin hands

>ROBBIE *at the hospital. He makes a call on his mobile. The phone rings in the flat.* ROBBIE *walks into the scene.*

CONNIE DEAN. oh shit that'll be him

SWIZ MURDOCK. fuck him leave it

CONNIE DEAN. can't leave it – fuck – don't say anything

SWIZ MURDOCK. aye

CONNIE DEAN. don't fuckin say anything

SWIZ MURDOCK. stay cool dear

>CONNIE *answers the phone.*

ROBBIE MULLIN. what kept ya

CONNIE DEAN. nothing – nothing – packin

ROBBIE MULLIN. everythin all right

CONNIE DEAN. just sortin some clothes out robbie – just sortin some clothes out

ROBBIE MULLIN. those wee lads still hangin about outside

CONNIE DEAN. they're away – no one about out there now – away

ROBBIE MULLIN. if the come back let me know

CONNIE DEAN. of course robbie a will

ROBBIE MULLIN. of course ya will – ya let me know everything don't ya

CONNIE DEAN. yes robbie

ROBBIE MULLIN. can't have people lying to me sure a can't

CONNIE DEAN. no robbie

ROBBIE MULLIN. can't have lies

CONNIE DEAN. no

ROBBIE MULLIN. called into that shop nearby earlier – got some bags – nice man owns that place – tellin me about

some spaced out junkie type in his shop this mornin –
bought a lot of chocolate

CONNIE DEAN. robbie a just needed a walk – there was
nothin to eat

ROBBIE MULLIN. don't speak

CONNIE DEAN. a didn't

ROBBIE MULLIN. now listen to me – take no more gear –
not a tablet not a joint not a fuckin drink – nothing – just
stand beside that window and look out on to the street – i'll
be back soon

ROBBIE *exits.*

SWIZ MURDOCK. what about another spliff

CONNIE DEAN. both of ya have to go now

SWIZ MURDOCK. given ya grief over the phone – fuck him

CONNIE DEAN. he'll be back soon – just go

SWIZ MURDOCK. sort him out – bop beat him with his big
hands

CONNIE *gets money from her purse.*

CONNIE DEAN (*to* SWIZ). here look take that

SWIZ MURDOCK. what's that for

CONNIE DEAN. just take it and leave – just take the money
and leave

SWIZ MURDOCK. what about later

CONNIE DEAN (*screaming*). get out – get fuckin out

9

THERESA's *office is empty.* DAVE *is sitting on a grass bank.
He is surrounded by the noise of heavy machinery, diggers etc.
THERESA enters the office and sits at her desk. There is a
message on her answering machine.*

DAVE BLACK. theresa it's me – listen love i'm sorry about earlier on – a didn't mean what a said – a know ya care – today's a bad day that's all – you're doin yer best at work a know that – none of that's easy – it's just – a don't know – i can't do anything here – a spoke with the police and that – there's nothing can be done the say – they've been told to finish at midnight tonight – he was nice about it this guy – that's not an easy job either – they've been told what to do and that's that – not bein able to do anything is the part a can't take – havin no control when ya feel ya should be doin something – i'm goin to stay here a while longer – have this feeling that a should – the workmen gave me a few sandwiches so i'm alright that way – police told me if the got more information the would act on it – not that that's likely – but ya never know – it's a nice day here – the sun's shining – a had this thought that no matter where he was buried i hoped the sun was shining – that would keep the earth warm – he wouldn't be lying in the cold ground – everybody's doin there best – right – anyway – you don't have to phone me back – i'll let ya know when i'm comin home – somebody here can give me a lift – talk to ya later – and don't worry theresa it's alright

10

BOP *and* SWIZ *in the street outside the flat.*

SWIZ MURDOCK. fuckin header – hear the screams of her

BOP TORBETT. i liked her

SWIZ MURDOCK. look at that – she gave me a score – give ya a tenner of it later on

BOP TORBETT. a score

SWIZ MURDOCK. aye – a know – fuckin eejit (*Jangles keys.*)

BOP TORBETT. you lift those

SWIZ MURDOCK. on the way out

BOP TORBETT. what ya goin do with them

SWIZ MURDOCK. give them to my brother – wire him off
they're doin a runner tonight

11

The shop. SAMMY *is behind the counter.* MAGGIE *and*
COOPER *are at the other end of the shop.*

COOPER JONES. ya want a bottle a this

MAGGIE LYTTLE. no

COOPER JONES. stick one in yer bag

MAGGIE LYTTLE. no

COOPER JONES. lapper

SAMMY LENNON. what's goin on down there

MAGGIE LYTTLE. go an pay for it

COOPER JONES. watch this (*At counter.*) what's yer panic –
do you not want me to buy somethin

SAMMY LENNON. were you in here earlier on – you an
another one

COOPER JONES. me – in here – no – i've been helpin my old
granny to do her shoppin all day – she has to walk all the
way to supermarket cause she says you're too dear – a
robber without a mask she says you are

SAMMY LENNON. you were in here an ya lifted sweets an
run out

COOPER JONES. a was with my granny i told you that

SAMMY LENNON. yer barred – put that back an get out

COOPER *opens the bottle and drinks.*

you'll have to pay for that

MAGGIE LYTTLE. cooper – let's go

COOPER JONES (*pours the rest of the bottle on the floor*).
no wonder my granny doesn't come in here (*He pretends to*

throw the bottle at SAMMY, SAMMY *is startled,*
COOPER *laughs*.)

SAMMY LENNON. i'm warnin ya don't come back

COOPER JONES. don't fuckin warn me

COOPER *lifts a bottle of water while him and* MAGGIE
exit. They stand outside the shop.

MAGGIE LYTTLE. grow up for christ sake

COOPER JONES. i'm only messing – i'll go back in an pay
him for the water

MAGGIE LYTTLE. stop pesterin him

COOPER JONES. ya want a drink a this (*She takes a drink.*)
ya goin go to the club tonight

MAGGIE LYTTLE. don't know

COOPER JONES. go on go – i want ya to go

MAGGIE LYTTLE. do we have to go – can we not do
somethin else

COOPER JONES. like what

MAGGIE LYTTLE. i don't know there must be something else
to do – go to the pictures

COOPER JONES. what for

MAGGIE LYTTLE. to see a movie

COOPER JONES. what ya wanna see a movie for – goin out
an just sittin there watchin somethin – i don't get that

MAGGIE LYTTLE. it's just somethin to do

COOPER JONES. go to the club – have a laugh – that's doin
somethin – that other thing it's just borin – watchin other
people do things – somebody makes up a story about people
in america and you sit an watch it – what's the point in that

MAGGIE LYTTLE. no point yer're right

COOPER JONES. a need to be hangin about the place anyway
– might need me on the door or somethin

MAGGIE LYTTLE. i'll go myself

COOPER JONES. to the pictures

MAGGIE LYTTLE. yes

COOPER JONES. on yer own

MAGGIE LYTTLE. by myself – on my own

COOPER JONES. tonight

MAGGIE LYTTLE. aye

COOPER JONES. who goes to the pictures on their own – no one

MAGGIE LYTTLE. i'll start a new craze

COOPER JONES. do what ever ya want then

MAGGIE LYTTLE. a will do whatever a want

COOPER JONES. a know ya will – that's cool

MAGGIE LYTTLE. a don't need you to tell me what to do

COOPER JONES. a didn't tell ya to do anythin

MAGGIE LYTTLE. do what ya want – go to the pictures – like you were givin me permission

COOPER JONES. i'm goin to the club that's what i'm doin

MAGGIE LYTTLE. a know that

COOPER JONES. a don't understan – what

MAGGIE LYTTLE. nothin

COOPER JONES. what

MAGGIE LYTTLE. nothin

COOPER JONES. i'll go to the pictures next week

MAGGIE LYTTLE. a don't want ya to go now

COOPER JONES. didn't ya just say

MAGGIE LYTTLE. a want to go on my own

COOPER JONES. have i done somethin here

MAGGIE LYTTLE. no

COOPER JONES. somethin a don't know about

MAGGIE LYTTLE. nothin ya don't know about

COOPER JONES. only a bit of a laugh ya know

SAMMY *enters brandishing a club.*

SAMMY LENNON. get away from here – go on move on

COOPER JONES. i'll pay for the water

SAMMY LENNON. i don't want yer money – just get away from my shop – i'll hit ya with this – i'm warnin ya

COOPER JONES (*laughs.*) you hit me with that (*To* MAGGIE.) mon we'll go

MAGGIE LYTTLE. i'm goin home

COOPER JONES. you'll be about later – on the corner – i'll see ya later

MAGGIE LYTTLE. maybe

12

The backyard of the pub. The inside of the pub is also visible but it is just background. HELEN *is kneeling in front of* JOE. *She stands up.* JOE *fixes his trousers.*

JOE HYNES. i need to get back to work

HELEN WOODS. jesus joe you can wait a few minutes surely

JOE HYNES. a few minutes – it's just over there everything's – dodgy

HELEN WOODS. i bought you somethin

JOE HYNES. a haven't forgotten somethin have a

HELEN WOODS. ya haven't forgotten anythin – a just wanted to buy ya somethin that's all – last ya a lifetime apparently – here

JOE HYNES (*smiles*). right

HELEN WOODS. ya not like it

JOE HYNES. no it's lovely

HELEN WOODS. have ya already got one – i'll get it changed – i only got it round the corner

JOE HYNES. i've stopped smokin – maeve's idea – well we've both been talkin about it

HELEN WOODS. you and her decided

JOE HYNES. aye – it's her really

HELEN WOODS (*lights a cigarette*). ya never mentioned anythin about it

JOE HYNES. the lighter's lovely – she read somewhere that smokin might damage yer sperm

HELEN WOODS (*offers him a cigarette*). ya haven't stopped then – you've just told her you've stopped

JOE HYNES. no a have

HELEN WOODS. take it

JOE HYNES. i've stopped

HELEN WOODS. i like you smokin

JOE HYNES. there must be other things about me helen

HELEN WOODS. i like lookin at ya smoke – the way ya smoke – i like it

JOE HYNES. well i'm sorry but what can a do

HELEN WOODS. tell her ya don't want to stop

JOE HYNES. but a do

HELEN WOODS. a thought ya said it was her makin ya

JOE HYNES. it's the right thing to do

HELEN WOODS. so it's you – you want to do it

JOE HYNES. humpin meat all day – haven't a fuckin breath left in me

HELEN WOODS. ya should've said

JOE HYNES. a didn't know about the lighter

HELEN WOODS. that's not it

JOE HYNES. what then

HELEN WOODS. we should've talked about it – not you an her you an me

JOE HYNES. i'll keep the lighter in case a start up again – which the way things are goin could be soon

HELEN WOODS. i'll bring it back

JOE HYNES. no a want to keep it – was she in the shop when ya were buyin it

HELEN WOODS. yeah

JOE HYNES. fuck

HELEN WOODS. what

JOE HYNES. nothin – i'm just thinkin the two a you together – a bit close like isn't it

HELEN WOODS. i didn't like bein there in her company – it didn't feel right

JOE HYNES. yer bound to bump into her now an again

HELEN WOODS. i don't like it

JOE HYNES. what do ya want me to do

HELEN WOODS. a don't know

JOE HYNES. ya don't want me to leave her

HELEN WOODS. would ya leave her

JOE HYNES. a don't know

HELEN WOODS. that's why i don't want you to do it

JOE HYNES. it's not the right time

HELEN WOODS. jesus christ – when is the right time

JOE HYNES. me leavin might put her over the edge

SHARON LAWTHER (*shouts from pub*). can we get some service here please – there's people's eyes hangin out with thirst

HELEN WOODS. a better go back in here

JOE HYNES. i'll call back over later

HELEN WOODS. aye

JOE HYNES. do ya want the lighter back – it's just maybe with me not smokin and her bein in the shop when ya bought it – if she saw it – ya know – she might – ya know

HELEN WOODS. no that's fine – i'll bring it back – better go out the back way – don't want ya walkin through the pub

JOE HYNES. nah

> JOE *exits.* HELEN *lights another cigarette.*

13

The flat. ROBBIE *is punching* CONNIE. *Throughout the beating* CONNIE *is silent. It is something she has gotten used to.*

14

A busy street. BETTY *is trying to cross the street. She is confused. She drops her handbag and the contents spill out. She kneels down to pick them up.*

ACT THREE

The end of the day.

1

The pub. HELEN *is behind the bar serving* FRANK COIN.
HARRY *and* PAUL *are standing at the counter.* BOBBIE,
SHANKS *and* SHARON *are at a table. She is drunk, she is
resting her head on the table.*

HELEN WOODS (*giving* FRANK *his pint*). there ya go –
    didn't a tell ya there was one waiting on ya

FRANK COIN. an a few more on top a that

HELEN WOODS. out walkin today

FRANK COIN. usual

HELEN WOODS. beautiful day for it

FRANK COIN. it was

    FRANK *sits at a table away from the rest.*

HARRY FOGGARTY (*to* HELEN). tins dear

HELEN WOODS. how many you want

HARRY FOGGARTY (*to* PAUL). how many we want

PAUL FOGGARTY. ten

HARRY FOGGARTY (*to* HELEN). give us a dozen

PAUL FOGGARTY. couldn't be ten

HARRY FOGGARTY. i'll square up for this

PAUL FOGGARTY. ya will not

HARRY FOGGARTY. let me do this

PAUL FOGGARTY. i'll get for the sandwiches then

HARRY FOGGARTY. right

> *They pay for the tins and sandwiches.*

> (*To* HELEN.) good job (*To* BOBBIE *etc.*) we're away on here

BOBBIE TORBETT. right – it was a good day – yer da was well looked after – (*To* HARRY.) that other thing earlier – sorry – a few drinks ya know

HARRY FOGGARTY. forgotten about

PAUL FOGGARTY. thanks for makin the effort – not to be forgotten

BOBBIE TORBETT. had to be done

SHANKS O'NEILL. good day – good send off

HARRY FOGGARTY. been better if there was more at it

PAUL FOGGARTY. aye

SHANKS O'NEILL (*to* PAUL). a wee word in yer ear there

PAUL FOGGARTY (*to* HARRY). you go on out i'll see ya out there

> HARRY *exits.*

SHANKS O'NEILL. god rest yer da an that y'know

PAUL FOGGARTY. aye

SHANKS O'NEILL. i'm stuck for a few quid – any chance ya could – y'know – drop us somethin – bad timin but – y'know

PAUL FOGGARTY. death put things in perspective

SHANKS O'NEILL. perspective aye

PAUL FOGGARTY. a tenner do ya

SHANKS O'NEILL. plenty

PAUL FOGGARTY. can't bring it with ye

SHANKS O'NEILL. yer a gentleman

> PAUL *exits.* SHANKS *returns to table.*

BOBBIE TORBETT. man's just buried his father

SHANKS O'NEILL. no better time

SHARON LAWTHER. get me somethin to eat bobbie

SHANKS O'NEILL. hang on in there darlin

BOBBIE TORBETT (*about* SHARON). see what a mean

SHANKS O'NEILL. she's alright

SHARON LAWTHER. we'll go back to the house bobbie an i'll cook something – i can cook ya know – don't think a can't a can

BOBBIE TORBETT. we're havin a drink

SHARON LAWTHER. cook with the best a them

> BOP *enters. He stands at the bar.* BOBBIE *walks over to* BOP.

BOBBIE TORBETT. ya been round to the house – get somethin to eat

BOP TORBETT. i'm alright

BOBBIE TORBETT. want a pint – sit down with us have a pint

BOP TORBETT. sit with them two

BOBBIE TORBETT. wise move – shouldn't be here myself

BOP TORBETT. go on home then

BOBBIE TORBETT. aye – i'll be headin round soon

BOP TORBETT. a left somethin on the pan for ya

BOBBIE TORBETT. right

BOP TORBETT. did ya ask for me

BOBBIE TORBETT. a did

BOP TORBETT. well what the say

BOBBIE TORBETT. there's nothin on at the moment – an the way things are lookin that's goin to be the case for a good while – sorry but that's what the said son

BOP TORBETT. they're not takin anybody on

BOBBIE TORBETT. there's other types a work son – it doesn't have to be that

BOP TORBETT. who were ya talkin to

BOBBIE TORBETT. who was a talkin to – fuck it – i'm not doin this – i'm not doin it – a wasn't talkin to anybody – the abattoir's a kip

BOP TORBETT. go sit down with yer mates an get drunk

BOBBIE *grabs* BOP *then lets him go.* BOP *exits.*

BOBBIE TORBETT. jesus – just tryin to explain somethin – should've sat down an had a drink – a could a explained something

He sits down at the table.

(*To* SHANKS.) go up an get a drink

SHANKS *goes to the bar.*

SHARON LAWTHER. i'd have made a good mother ya know bobbie – plenty of love in me – people don't see that but it's there – you see it bobbie don't ya

BOBBIE TORBETT. aye

2

The abattoir. THERESA *is in her office. The fire alarm is ringing.* THERESA *is putting her coat on.* JOE *enters carrying a football.*

JOE HYNES. it's not the real thing – one a the lads smashed the glass with the ball

THERESA BLACK. i was goin to call ya up anyway – he signed the contract – everything's clear for a month

The alarm stops.

JOE HYNES. a month

THERESA BLACK. that's as long term as he could get – i'll get these cheques signed (*Signing cheques.*) get everyone away home – he said he wants a meetin with ya first thing monday mornin

JOE HYNES. a meetin about what

THERESA BLACK. there was no details joe – all he said was there's goin to have to be changes – a don't care – today's been sorted out that's all i'm interested in

JOE HYNES. short term contracts

THERESA BLACK. he didn't say that's what it was

JOE HYNES. changes he said

THERESA BLACK. changes

JOE HYNES. that's what it is

THERESA BLACK. once i've all these signed will ya give them out – a don't want them all comin up here

JOE HYNES. aye sure – ya alright

THERESA BLACK. bit of a headache just

JOE HYNES. changes – that could mean fuckin anythin – turn the whole lot into a packin plant – that's half a them laid off – either that or the short term contracts – either way it's walkin time – no big bucks for him then

THERESA BLACK. there is no big bucks joe

JOE HYNES. he doesn't keep this place goin for the love of it

THERESA BLACK. he's not makin a fortune – i have a feelin given half a chance he'd close the place – he's never happy

JOE HYNES. who is – there's not many in here wake up in the mornin kissin the sunshine

THERESA BLACK. i'm just sayin joe – from talkin to him i think he's had enough

JOE HYNES. fuck him i've had enough

THERESA BLACK. we've all had enough – we don't own the place though do we – us havin enough means a shoutin

match in the house or an extra pint on the way home – him
havin enough means the place closes – wait until monday

JOE HYNES. fuck it – yer right – monday mornin's a long
time away – know what a think

THERESA BLACK. no joe tell me what ya think

JOE HYNES. you don't care what a think do ya

THERESA BLACK. not really no – but tell me anyway

JOE HYNES. i think we have as much control over what
happens as the lumps a dead meat we carry about the place

THERESA BLACK. i think yer right

JOE HYNES. i know i'm right – see when a started here know
the only thing a had on my mind – say no a don't joe –
cause a bet ya ya don't know what it is

THERESA BLACK. no a don't joe

JOE HYNES. the only thing a had on my mind was losin
weight

THERESA BLACK. an look at you now it's worked

JOE HYNES. it has – ya know my wife don't ya – maeve

THERESA BLACK. i've met her – lovely girl

JOE HYNES. lovely girl – i always fancied maeve – but she
never seemed too keen – and i got it into my head it was
because a was too fat – so in order to get her round to my
way of thinkin a thought i'll have to drop the weight – a
mate a mine says get a job in the abattoir the weight'll fall
of ye – that's why i'm here – over ten years ago that was –
an it worked because a got the girl – funny as fuck how
things work out isn't it

THERESA BLACK. i'm bustin my sides

JOE HYNES. you could put a sofa in here an charge people –
yer a good listener

THERESA BLACK. go down an give the cheques out

JOE HYNES. know what i'm thinkin – know what would
happen if i didn't weigh in on monday mornin

THERESA BLACK. what

JOE HYNES. fuck all – that's what would happen – i'm takin the wee lad's cheque

THERESA BLACK. aye

> JOE *exits*. THERESA *signs a cheque then folds it and puts it in her handbag. She takes a hand mirror from her bag and studies her face in it.*

3

The shop. SAMMY *is behind the counter. He is about to make a phone call.* BETTY *enters.* SAMMY *puts the phone down.*

SAMMY LENNON. where have ya been – i was just about to phone the police betty – what happened

BETTY LENNON. nothing happened

SAMMY LENNON. a thought something had happened to ya

BETTY LENNON. i bought some clothes that's all – a dress – a bought a new dress

SAMMY LENNON. why didn't ya phone me – ya could've phoned me betty

BETTY LENNON (*takes dress from bag*). do ya like the dress

SAMMY LENNON. it's lovely

BETTY LENNON. do ya like the dress – it took me a long time to pick this dress – do ya like it – look at it

SAMMY LENNON. yes a like the dress

BETTY LENNON. it'll suit me won't it – it's the type a thing i look well in

SAMMY LENNON. you should've phoned

BETTY LENNON. stop being an old fool

SAMMY LENNON. i was worried – what happened at the hospital – i thought maybe ya got bad news or somethin and ya went off somewhere

BETTY LENNON. where would a go sammy

SAMMY LENNON. i don't know – what happened

BETTY LENNON. it's fine – everything's fine

SAMMY LENNON. what did the doctor say

BETTY LENNON. she said everything's fine

SAMMY LENNON. and have ya to go back or anything

BETTY LENNON. did the rest of the order arrive

SAMMY LENNON. he was here – tried to pull another fast one – a box of crisps he said we already had

BETTY LENNON. ya checked everythin then

SAMMY LENNON. double checked it – you'll not be pullin any fast ones here i said to him

BETTY LENNON. what he say

SAMMY LENNON. what could he say

BETTY LENNON. maybe we should sell up

SAMMY LENNON. need to get one of those alarm systems in first – anybody buyin the place would expect it – a phoned up about them – there's a fella comin out tomorrow

BETTY LENNON. that type of thing might be costly sammy

SAMMY LENNON. if it's too costly (*Takes out the club from under the counter.*) this is plan b

BETTY LENNON. don't be stupid

SAMMY LENNON. it worked today – one of those hoods was in the place – they're barred – it's the only type a behaviour the understand betty – he was goin to throw a bottle at me – i let him know though – told them not to come back – their business wasn't wanted here – chased him off with this – the have to know ya mean business

BETTY LENNON. put it back upstairs

SAMMY LENNON. a will not – it's stayin behind the counter

BETTY LENNON. i'm goin to phone up an get somebody round to value the place

SAMMY LENNON. the shop and the house – we sell the house we'll have to buy another

BETTY LENNON. unless we want to live in the street we would

SAMMY LENNON. where would we go

BETTY LENNON. move up the road a bit

SAMMY LENNON. those houses are too big for us – wouldn't have the money for one of those even if the weren't too big

BETTY LENNON. they're buildin smaller ones round the corner from the bigger ones

SAMMY LENNON. new houses betty – what would we want with a new house

BETTY LENNON. we'll see – talk about it later

SAMMY LENNON. aye – see the type a money involved – this place mightn't be worth as much as we think

BETTY LENNON. maybe – i'm goin up to lie down – you be alright here on yer own

SAMMY LENNON. me and my friend here will keep things tickin over

BETTY LENNON. sammy a don't want ya

SAMMY LENNON. i'm only jokin – go have yer lie down – know what a was thinkin

BETTY LENNON. what

SAMMY LENNON. i'll cook us both a nice meal tonight – we haven't done that in a while

BETTY LENNON. no we haven't

SAMMY LENNON. i'll cook us both a nice meal later on – after you've had yer sleep – maybe close the place a bit early tonight

BETTY LENNON. that would be nice

SAMMY LENNON. aye it would

4

The allotment. PAUL *and* HARRY *are drinking tins of beer.*

HARRY FOGGARTY. cheers

PAUL FOGGARTY. good luck

HARRY FOGGARTY. god rest ya da

PAUL FOGGARTY. god rest him – still can't work out why he did that – let the two of us think he got rid a this place

HARRY FOGGARTY. there's plenty a things ya don't know about people isn't there

PAUL FOGGARTY. think he was tellin us something

HARRY FOGGARTY. what way – he wasn'e one a the world's thinkers was he

PAUL FOGGARTY. just tryin to work this out

HARRY FOGGARTY. there is no workin out to it – he just wanted the place to himself – see inside the shed's still the same

PAUL FOGGARTY. is it

HARRY FOGGARTY. everything fuckin perfect – spotless

PAUL FOGGARTY. i hated the way he made us scrub everything clean

HARRY FOGGARTY. in order to do a job right what have ya got to look after

PAUL FOGGARTY. you've got to look after yer tools

HARRY FOGGARTY. a fuckin surgeon's tools wouldn't be as clean as those

PAUL FOGGARTY. he loved this place

HARRY FOGGARTY. a savin grace for people that don't say much

PAUL FOGGARTY. my ma god rest her was never up here

HARRY FOGGARTY. never

PAUL FOGGARTY. he wouldn't let her come up

HARRY FOGGARTY. she wouldn't have come up anyway –
the house was hers the allotment was his

PAUL FOGGARTY. don't think she was too keen on us comin
up here y'know

HARRY FOGGARTY. she didn't give a fuck

PAUL FOGGARTY. don't know

HARRY FOGGARTY. my da's shed – member yer wee
woman – daly ya called her – buck teeth dirty fingernails –
her da had to go on the run at some stage or somethin

PAUL FOGGARTY. aye – him an my da were mates were the
not

HARRY FOGGARTY. aye – member her

PAUL FOGGARTY. a do

HARRY FOGGARTY. me an her used to go at it some steam
in that shed – some girl she was

PAUL FOGGARTY. i know that

HARRY FOGGARTY. how'd ya know that

PAUL FOGGARTY. she told me

HARRY FOGGARTY. told ya when

PAUL FOGGARTY. told me when me an her were goin at it
some steam in the shed

HARRY FOGGARTY. ya never said

PAUL FOGGARTY. what would a say for

HARRY FOGGARTY. dirty bastard – i liked her – don't like
her now cause she did the dirty on me – liked her then
though – you did that on me

PAUL FOGGARTY. what about you and the home brew

HARRY FOGGARTY. the home brew was good – better than
this shite – that was a different matter

PAUL FOGGARTY. how was it a different matter

HARRY FOGGARTY. my da assumed it was yers – i didn't do the dirty on ya – stealin someone's girl is doin the dirty

PAUL FOGGARTY. she wasn't yer girl – wasn't she goin out with yer man brennan – brother only had one hand – the only reason my da assumed it was me was because ya told him it was me

HARRY FOGGARTY. he must've thought you looked like a drinker or somethin

PAUL FOGGARTY. he beat the shite out a me for that

HARRY FOGGARTY. beat the shite out a the two of us for plenty a things

PAUL FOGGARTY. whenever he went for the belt ya knew it was serious

HARRY FOGGARTY. there was a few times he was very nearly gettin fuckin choked with it

PAUL FOGGARTY. felt like that myself – member i poured the weedkiller over the roses – fuck

HARRY FOGGARTY. never seen him like that – thought the tears were goin burst out a him

PAUL FOGGARTY. standin there lookin at the rose bush – ya thought somebody had just fuckin died – not a word out a him – he didn't speak to me for weeks – see just where yer sittin – right where those weeds are – what we goin to do with this place then

HARRY FOGGARTY. it's not like we can divide it up or anythin is it

PAUL FOGGARTY. not like him to let weeds grow

HARRY FOGGARTY. aye – sell it

PAUL FOGGARTY. ya want to do that

HARRY FOGGARTY. don't think so

PAUL FOGGARTY. either we look after it or we let it go

HARRY FOGGARTY. ya look after the gardenin part of it right – and i'll use the shed for women

PAUL FOGGARTY. what women

HARRY FOGGARTY. some women

PAUL FOGGARTY. no women

HARRY FOGGARTY. right scrub the shed idea then

PAUL FOGGARTY. listen – when somebody dies ya bury them

HARRY FOGGARTY. easiest way i'm told

PAUL FOGGARTY. that's like death – buryin is death –
    something's dead there's no growth – what about burial
    with growth – in memory of my da know what i'm sayin

HARRY FOGGARTY. no

PAUL FOGGARTY. dig those weeds up and plant some
    flowers – my da's flowers

HARRY FOGGARTY. now

PAUL FOGGARTY. yes certainly now – on the day he was
    buried ya see it has to be done today like – before midnight
    – the day he was buried

HARRY FOGGARTY. the day he was buried – yer not usin
    my shovel by the way

PAUL FOGGARTY. what one's that

HARRY FOGGARTY. the one with the black handle

PAUL FOGGARTY. that one's mine

HARRY FOGGARTY. fuckin sure it's not

PAUL FOGGARTY. fuckin sure it is

5

The flat. CONNIE *is putting make-up on her bruised face.*
ROBBIE *is finishing the packing. He sets a shoulder bag
beside* CONNIE.

ROBBIE MULLIN. the gear is in that bag – you look after it –
    don't let it out a yer sight – an don't be dippin into it either

(*Takes a bag of pills from the shoulder bag.*) here take that (*She doesn't move.*) take it – have them on the way down if ya want

ROBBIE *exits to the bedroom.*CONNIE *takes a pill and puts the rest in her handbag. She continues to put make-up on. It is painful.* ROBBIE *enters with a wad of money.*

ten grand roughly – that's our lot – put it in yer handbag

CONNIE DEAN. we need to stop at a chemist – i need more make up (*He touches her face she pulls away.*) you'll have to go in and get it – i'll tell ya what to get

ROBBIE MULLIN. right – there'll be somewhere on the way out – get it in a garage would ya

CONNIE DEAN. no

ROBBIE MULLIN. we'll find somewhere – are ya nearly ready – we need to get goin a don't want to be drivin all night

CONNIE DEAN. ya want me to look my best don't ya – this takes time

ROBBIE MULLIN. ya want a drink

CONNIE DEAN. no

ROBBIE MULLIN (*getting a drink*). give the ole doll that runs the shop a lift to the hospital today – her husband talkin away to me about hoods breakin into his shop – he says they're all high on drugs – then he says he's worried about his wife getting a taxi because he thinks they're all drug dealers – so a give her a lift in a car full a gear – people haven't a fuckin clue have the

SPILO JOHNSTON *and* RAT JOYCE *walk into the room. They are gunmen.*

SPILO JOHNSTON. neither one a you say a word

ROBBIE MULLIN. i've money ya can take it – i'm movin out anyway there's no need

SPILO JOHNSTON. a just told ya not to speak – don't say a fuckin word – kneel down in the middle a the floor

ROBBIE MULLIN. jesus don't

SPILO JOHNSTON. ya speak again an i'm goin to put one in
yer napper right now – (ROBBIE *kneels*.) we need a tie an a
hankie (*To* CONNIE.) hey you turn round – what happened
to yer face

CONNIE DEAN. nothin

SPILO JOHNSTON. he do that to ya – yer some fella aren't ya
(*to* CONNIE.) get me a hankie an a tie

CONNIE *exits to the bedroom followed by* RAT JOYCE.
SPILO *looks about the room, checks the CDs etc.* CONNIE
and RAT *enter.* SPILO *stuffs the hankie in* ROBBIE*'s mouth
and ties his hands behind his back.*

SPILO JOHNSTON. that's better – (*To* CONNIE.) nobody
mentioned you – sit down – don't panic just listen – (*He
talks to her with his gun.*) ya listenin

CONNIE DEAN. yes

SPILO JOHNSTON. good – yer gonna take whatever bag
belongs to ya and go – yer not to come back here ya
understan

CONNIE DEAN. yes

SPILO JOHNSTON. yer seen round here again yer goin to end
up the same way as him – when ya leave ya speak to no one
ya got that

CONNIE DEAN. yes

SPILO JOHNSTON. a don't know what ya think of this scum-
bag here – personally speakin if he did that to my face a
wouldn't be too happy with him – the point is – phonin the
peelers isn't goin to do him any good but it'll do you a lot a
harm – and don't think we won't be able to find ya we will
– ya understan all that

CONNIE DEAN. yes

SPILO JOHNSTON. well take yer stuff and away ya go

CONNIE *lifts her handbag and the shoulder bag. She
stands beside* ROBBIE.

CONNIE DEAN. can a hit him

SPILO JOHNSTON. only i've to do what i've been told i'd let you shoot him – welt away

CONNIE DEAN. bastard

CONNIE *punches* ROBBIE *and spits on him. She exits.*

SPILO JOHNSTON. she certainly doesn't like you – couldn't blame her – i've been told to tell ya this is a warnin – you want to be the man in the big picture shoutin yer head off – sayin things ya shouldn't say – i'd advise ya to do it somewhere else – but ya know that – bags packed an everything – too late – what a bummer (*He pushes* ROBBIE *to the ground and rolls him over face down.*) hold his legs down (RAT *does this.* SPILO *shoots* ROBBIE *in the back of both knees. He is going to shoot him in the ankles but the gun jams.*) give me yers (*Gives him the gun.*) you ever do this before

RAT JOYCE. no

SPILO JOHNSTON. away ya go then

RAT *shoots* ROBBIE *in both ankles. They exit.*

6

The pub. HELEN *is behind the counter. She is flicking the lid of the lighter open and closed while looking at her mobile phone which she has in her hand.* FRANK, BOBBIE, SHANKS *and* SHARON *are at their usual tables.* JOE *is in the abattoir, he is changing out of his work clothes.* MAEVE *is at home. There is a cot in the room. A baby is crying.* MAEVE *lifts the baby from the cot to stop it crying.* FRANK *walks from his table to the counter.*

FRANK COIN (*to* HELEN). waitin on a call

HELEN WOODS. thinkin a makin one

FRANK COIN. always better off makin them than not

HELEN WOODS. time for a half un is it

FRANK COIN. that time alright

> HELEN *gets* FRANK *his drink and he sits down at his table.* HELEN *makes a call.* JOE *is in the abattoir. His phone rings.* HELEN *walks into the scene.*

HELEN WOODS. hello

JOE HYNES. how's it goin (*Silence.*) hello are ya there

HELEN WOODS. yeah i'm here

JOE HYNES. i'll be over soon

HELEN WOODS. i'm goin home joe

JOE HYNES. that's alright i'll meet ya round at yer place then

HELEN WOODS. a was thinkin of havin an early night – on my feet all day

JOE HYNES. ya not want me to come round

HELEN WOODS. a don't think so

> MAEVE *is nursing the baby. She makes a phone call. She walks into the scene.*

JOE HYNES. hold on a minute there's somebody beepin me – hold on – hello

MAEVE HYNES. where are ya

JOE HYNES. where do ya think a am i'm at work

MAEVE HYNES. a wee baby boy – she had a wee baby boy – nine poun something – looks just like her

JOE HYNES. maeve i've a union guy holdin on here

MAEVE HYNES. how'd it go today

JOE HYNES. hold on a minute – ya still there

HELEN WOODS. yes

JOE HYNES. maeve's on the other line

HELEN WOODS. i'll just go on then joe

JOE HYNES. no no wait – i'll get rid of her just wait – hello – a can't stay on here

MAEVE HYNES. tell me how it went

JOE HYNES. it's sorted out

MAEVE HYNES. that's good – ya want to see the baby joe it's beautiful

JOE HYNES. a have to go

MAEVE HYNES. when are ya comin home

JOE HYNES. don't know

MAEVE HYNES. you'll not be long i've a surprise for ya

JOE HYNES. what

MAEVE HYNES. you'll see when ya get here

JOE HYNES. it didn't cost money did it

MAEVE HYNES. not a penny joe

JOE HYNES. right

MAEVE HYNES. don't be long

   MAEVE *exits*.

JOE HYNES. she's away (*Silence.*) a can't hear ya

HELEN WOODS. a didn't say anythin

JOE HYNES. i'll call over to the pub before ya go

HELEN WOODS. no don't

JOE HYNES. what's the matter

HELEN WOODS. nothin – just tired – i'm goin to go on here

JOE HYNES. phone me later

   HELEN *moves back into the pub and starts collecting glasses from the tables.* SHARON *returns to her seat from the toilet.*

SHANKS O'NEILL. don't ya feel better for that

SHARON LAWTHER. aye – give us a feg

SHANKS O'NEILL (*he does*). a told ya a good boke get it all out a yer system – isn't that right bobbie a good boke is the makins of ya on days like this

BOBBIE TORBETT. aye (*To* SHARON.) you alright

SHARON LAWTHER. do a look alright

BOBBIE TORBETT (*to* SHANKS). what ya call the barmaid

SHANKS O'NEILL. in here nearly everyday ya don't remember what ya call her

BOBBIE TORBETT. just tell me her fuckin name

SHANKS O'NEILL. helen her name's helen

BOBBIE TORBETT. have to have a word with her

SHANKS O'NEILL. buy another gargle when yer up there

BOBBIE TORBETT. i've had enough (*He moves to counter.*) helen

HELEN WOODS. same again

BOBBIE TORBETT. no – no more – is it alright if a have a word with you a minute

HELEN WOODS. i've no money on me

BOBBIE TORBETT. no not that – this mornin – when the world was a clearer place – i remember you sayin that ya were short staffed here or somethin

HELEN WOODS. why ya lookin a job

BOBBIE TORBETT. a don't think so – i have a wee lad – about eighteen he is – ya see him in earlier

HELEN WOODS. good lookin fella

BOBBIE TORBETT. takes after his ma – he's a good kid – he needs work – he's lookin a job in that fuckin kip across the way – can i tell you this – no good sayin to him he won't listen – i don't want him over there – you see – it does somethin to ya – i worked there all my days – start out as a kid – then workin there – talkin with men all the time – shoutin and slabberin – it hardens ya – i was the hardest man in that place – what use has it done me – none – only i'm minus a wife now – i don't want that for him – ya understand that – so is there any chance ya could fit him in here – least be a starter for him – not get him involved in that – would you do that

HELEN WOODS. can he start tomorrow

BOBBIE TORBETT. yer a darlin – here first thing he'll be – a darlin ya are

SHARON *stands beside* BOBBIE *at the bar.*

SHARON LAWTHER. ya want a drink

BOBBIE TORBETT. cheers helen luv – no – don't you be takin anymore

SHARON LAWTHER. i'm just havin this one (*To* HELEN.) a gin an a pint

HELEN *gets the drinks and* SHARON *pays for them.*

BOBBIE TORBETT. i'm drinkin whatever's there then i'm headin home

SHARON LAWTHER. ya not goin to ask me to go with ya

BOBBIE TORBETT. no – go round to yer sister's

SHARON LAWTHER. a wouldn't be welcome there

BOBBIE TORBETT. stayin with me sharon isn't goin to work out ya know that

SHARON LAWTHER. a don't know that

BOBBIE TORBETT. well i do – go back round to the flat an sort it out

SHARON LAWTHER. there is nothing to sort out

BOBBIE TORBETT. if he's gone all the better

SHARON LAWTHER. he was never there to go

BOBBIE TORBETT. never there what

SHARON LAWTHER. i live on my own bobbie – a have done this years

BOBBIE TORBETT. what was all that last night then

SHARON LAWTHER. didn't want to be on my own anymore that's all

BOBBIE TORBETT. what's in the suitcase

SHARON LAWTHER. nothing

BOBBIE TORBETT. jesus sharon luv – what the fuck

SHARON LAWTHER. there's times when i think about you
    bobbie an last night was one a them – thought we could
    spend a few days together see what might happen

BOBBIE TORBETT. nothing's goin to happen

SHARON LAWTHER. no

BOBBIE TORBETT. what ya goin to do

SHARON LAWTHER. sit an have a drink with shanks – he's
    an obnoxious little bollocks but better that then nothin

BOBBIE TORBETT. i'm not a fuckin expert on these matters
    but why don't ya try an straighten yerself out

SHARON LAWTHER. bobbie for fuck sake

BOBBIE TORBETT. a know

SHANKS O'NEILL. my mouth's dryin up here

SHARON LAWTHER. ya sittin down

BOBBIE TORBETT. just to finish what's in front a me – look
    after yerself

SHARON LAWTHER. yeah

They move to the table. SHARON *sits.* BOBBIE *stands.*

SHANKS O'NEILL. sit down there

BOBBIE TORBETT. i'm goin on here

SHANKS O'NEILL. goin on where

BOBBIE TORBETT. goin on home

SHANKS O'NEILL. we'll all go then

SHARON LAWTHER. no i'm not

BOBBIE TORBETT. i've to go home to my bed – you sit here
    with sharon keep her company

SHANKS O'NEILL. an what about after

BOBBIE TORBETT. go round to yer own house – i'm sure
    yer ma would like the company

SHARON LAWTHER. you live with yer ma

BOBBIE TORBETT. him an his ma have great fun together

SHARON LAWTHER (*laughing*). ya live with yer ma

7

The street. SWIZ, COOPER *and* BOP *are lively.*

COOPER JONES. moo

SWIZ MURDOCK. moo

COOPER JONES. mon bop give it a moo

BOP TORBETT. moo – moo – moo – moo

COOPER JONES. get some a these wee dolls round the club show them the business

SWIZ MURDOCK. wee dolls is it – you on yer own tonight – no lovely maggie bop

COOPER JONES. says she's away to the pictures – fuck it

SWIZ MURDOCK. what were the tales from the riverbank

COOPER JONES. moo

SWIZ MURDOCK. what

COOPER JONES. don't be sayin fuck all

SWIZ MURDOCK. rather eat my own eyes out

COOPER JONES. first time – fuckin beezer

SWIZ MURDOCK. first one in – hear that bop – cooper an maggie the pokey people

COOPER JONES. pokey man

SWIZ MURDOCK. any good

COOPER JONES. aye it was good

SWIZ MURDOCK. that's you in love now

BOP TORBETT. moo – moo – moo

COOPER JONES. yer right bop – bop's right

MAGGIE *enters*.

SWIZ MURDOCK. the maggie – no swim suit

MAGGIE LYTTLE. dick

SWIZ MURDOCK. moo dick

COOPER JONES. thought ya were headin off to the pictures –
couldn't stay away

MAGGIE LYTTLE. a went smart arse

COOPER JONES. the makin movies shorter these days

MAGGIE LYTTLE. the queue was too long

SWIZ MURDOCK. how'd the swimmin go maggie did ya
have a good time

MAGGIE LYTTLE. ya weren't there – work it out

SWIZ MURDOCK. cooper said he had a good time – we had a
good time bop didn't we

MAGGIE LYTTLE. standin here all day aye

SWIZ MURDOCK. oh no – where were we bop

BOP TORBETT. round at the druggies' flat

SWIZ MURDOCK. in the druggies' flat

COOPER JONES. doin what

SWIZ MURDOCK. doin who – that right bop doin who – isn't
that right bop

BOP TORBETT. aye

MAGGIE LYTTLE. you two – a don't think so

SWIZ MURDOCK. two of us standin outside the flat she
comes to the window – what happens next – gets the jugs
out – next thing in the jacuzzi

MAGGIE LYTTLE. aye dead on

SWIZ MURDOCK. bop am a right or wrong – tell them – go on

BOP TORBETT. we were round there

MAGGIE LYTTLE. in the jacuzzi with the druggie girl

SWIZ MURDOCK. bubbles up to our arses

COOPER JONES. the bop fella

SWIZ MURDOCK. everybody was in the water today – an what did yer uncle swiz get us (*Produces dope.*) a big chunk a blow – sky high for the water babies

COOPER JONES. chill out gear

SWIZ MURDOCK. chill out gear

COOPER JONES. the chill out gear maggie

MAGGIE LYTTLE. roll one up then

COOPER JONES. roll one up is right

SWIZ MURDOCK. i've no skins

COOPER JONES. you any

MAGGIE LYTTLE. i don't smoke what would a have them for

COOPER JONES. bop

BOP TORBETT. no

COOPER JONES. fuck that i'm not eatin it – a hate that it takes hours

MAGGIE LYTTLE. buy some

COOPER JONES. the shop – bop's the man for the shop – skins an water – this is the plan

SWIZ MURDOCK. plans are good

COOPER JONES. the old fucker barred me today so no money is to exchange hands here

MAGGIE LYTTLE. can we not just buy them

COOPER JONES. no

SWIZ MURDOCK. no is right

COOPER JONES. bop's on the team

SWIZ MURDOCK. no lappin the show like ya did last night

BOP TORBETT. a didn't

COOPER JONES. ya gonna do it

BOP TORBETT. aye what

COOPER JONES. give us all the money ya have

BOP TORBETT. what for

COOPER JONES. so we know ya didn't pay for them

BOP TORBETT. i'm not givin you two my money

COOPER JONES. i'm heart broken ya don't trust us –
    maggie'll look after it

SWIZ MURDOCK. he trusts the lovely maggie

  BOP *gives* MAGGIE *the money.*

  seven quid – not goin to do much damage with that

BOP TORBETT. you owe me a tenner

COOPER JONES. go forth an come back with water an skins

BOP TORBETT. the skins are behind the counter

COOPER JONES. there in lies the challenge

BOP TORBETT. i'll buy the skins an steal the water

COOPER JONES. no

MAGGIE LYTTLE. they're behind the counter – what is he
    invisible

SWIZ MURDOCK. he pretends he has a gun

BOP TORBETT. i'm not doin that

SWIZ MURDOCK. lappin the show

COOPER JONES. it's a joke that's all – stick yer finger in yer
    coat pocket – give it some verbals – then on yer way out the
    door take yer hand out a yer pocket an wave at him – what's
    the problem there – he'll even find that funny himself

BOP TORBETT. wave bye bye to him

COOPER JONES. wave bye bye to him

SWIZ MURDOCK. piece a piss – moo

BOP TORBETT. right i'll do it

SWIZ MURDOCK. moo chill out moo

MAGGIE LYTTLE. i'll go with him

COOPER JONES. he'll be alright on his own – you'll be
alright on yer own

BOP TORBETT. aye

8

The abattoir. THERESA's *office. She is sitting in the dark.*
DAVE *is standing in a field. The diggers have stopped. He
takes a few deep breaths then makes a phone call. The phone
rings in the office.* THERESA *turns the light on.* DAVE *walks
into the scene.* THERESA *answers the phone.*

THERESA BLACK. yes

DAVE BLACK. what are ya still doin there

THERESA BLACK. nothin – i'm leavin now – where are ya at
home

DAVE BLACK. no

THERESA BLACK. come on home dave – i need you to come
home

DAVE BLACK. they've found the body (*Silence.*) theresa did
you hear what a said they've found the body

THERESA BLACK. i heard – how can the be sure it's him

DAVE BLACK. it's him

THERESA BLACK. how can the be sure

DAVE BLACK. i recognise the shoes – it's his shoes (*Silence.*)
you alright

THERESA BLACK. i'm alright – how did the find him –
where was he – did the use a digger – it didn't hit him or
anything did it

DAVE BLACK. he was near a hedge that had grown there –
the dug him out with shovels – the can't move him just yet –
they're waitin on someone comin with a coffin

THERESA BLACK. put a blanket over him

DAVE BLACK. there is a blanket over him – when the coffin
comes the have to take him away for official identification

THERESA BLACK. his shoes

DAVE BLACK. i know – i'm goin to stay with him

THERESA BLACK. yes

DAVE BLACK. i got them to leave me alone with him – i –
i said a few prayers over him and told him that we loved
him – oh my god theresa (*Silence*.)

THERESA BLACK. it's alright dave

DAVE BLACK. it's not alright (*Pause*.) look there's no point in
ya doin anythin now – a know ya want to be here but
there's no point in comin down now – come down
tomorrow yeah

THERESA BLACK. yeah

DAVE BLACK. bring some of my clothes down would ya

THERESA BLACK. like what

DAVE BLACK. anything – somethin dark – look i'm goin to
have to go here – something's happenin a don't know –
maybe the coffins arrived or somethin – so i'm goin to go
alright

THERESA BLACK. yeah

DAVE BLACK. you alright

THERESA BLACK. yeah – i'll be down first thing in the
mornin

DAVE BLACK. the found him theresa – the found our boy

THERESA BLACK. go you on and get things sorted out dave
– i'll be down in the mornin

DAVE BLACK. right – don't be sittin there all night go home

THERESA BLACK. a will

DAVE BLACK. i'm away on

THERESA BLACK. right

DAVE *exits*. THERESA *is motionless*.

my baby (*Her scream is silent then she howls with grief.*)

9

The allotment. PAUL *and* HARRY *have stopped digging. They have found guns.*

PAUL FOGGARTY. guns – fuckin guns

HARRY FOGGARTY. want are ya lookin at me for i didn't put them there

PAUL FOGGARTY. what are the doin there

HARRY FOGGARTY. the mightn't be his

PAUL FOGGARTY. no that's right the mightn't be his – who put them there then the fuckin gun fairy

HARRY FOGGARTY. somebody else might a planked them

PAUL FOGGARTY. guns for what

HARRY FOGGARTY. shootin deer – that's why ya don't see any a them up round here – we live in belfast what do ya think the were for – they're in good nick

PAUL FOGGARTY. how ya know that

HARRY FOGGARTY. what do ya mean how do a know it

PAUL FOGGARTY. you seem to know a lot about them

HARRY FOGGARTY. a know nothing about them

PAUL FOGGARTY. are the yers

HARRY FOGGARTY. aye a brought ya up here to shoot ye – fuckin eejit – they're clean that's what a meant – spotless – well looked after

PAUL FOGGARTY. they're my da's then

HARRY FOGGARTY. he could a just been lookin after them for somebody – the knew he had an allotment – say the said look would ya bury them for a while – that happens

PAUL FOGGARTY. not that that's good – it's not – but if it's not that (HARRY *shrugs*.) what does shruggin yer shoulders mean

HARRY FOGGARTY. it means ya know as much as i do

PAUL FOGGARTY. if he wasn't keeping them for someone it means the were his

HARRY FOGGARTY. i know that

PAUL FOGGARTY. and if the were his what – he might a used them – in fact no might about it – if the were his he used them

HARRY FOGGARTY. he didn't use them

PAUL FOGGARTY. then what the fuck was he doin with them – and why were the buried

HARRY FOGGARTY. well it's not the wild west is it – ya hardly go around wearin them on yer fuckin holster

PAUL FOGGARTY. where's the joke here

HARRY FOGGARTY. the gun fairy – was that not a joke – an stop talking to me like that – buried guns or no fuckin buried you'll get a slap

PAUL FOGGARTY. what's wrong with you – get a slap – fuckin wise up – so my da's a murderer

HARRY FOGGARTY. don't be sayin that

PAUL FOGGARTY. it could be true

HARRY FOGGARTY. it's not true

PAUL FOGGARTY. how do ya know

HARRY FOGGARTY. he was my da for christ sake – a think i'd know if he was a murderer or not

PAUL FOGGARTY. ya didn't know he buried guns did ya

HARRY FOGGARTY. that's different

PAUL FOGGARTY. how's it different

HARRY FOGGARTY. anybody can bury guns only some can use them though

PAUL FOGGARTY. this is why he lied about the allotment

HARRY FOGGARTY. looks like it – solves the problem too of what we're goin to do with it

PAUL FOGGARTY. fuckin creates a problem

HARRY FOGGARTY. not for me it doesn't

PAUL FOGGARTY. it does for me

HARRY FOGGARTY. all we got a do is put them back where the were – let this place grow over an forget about it

PAUL FOGGARTY. forget about it

HARRY FOGGARTY. he's dead now there's not much we can do about that – not like we can ask him is it – even if we could it's hardly likely he'd tell ya – which must be part of the reason he stopped us from comin here

PAUL FOGGARTY. what

HARRY FOGGARTY. to protect us

PAUL FOGGARTY. to protect us – fuck that was big of him

HARRY FOGGARTY. yeah it was – whatever he was involved in he didn't want us to get involved in it in any way

PAUL FOGGARTY. does it not bother you that my da might a shot someone and in all likelihood the poor fucker that he shot is dead

HARRY FOGGARTY. a told ya stop talkin like that

PAUL FOGGARTY. not sayin it isn't goin to make it any less true is it

HARRY FOGGARTY. there's nothing we can do

PAUL FOGGARTY. yes there is

HARRY FOGGARTY. what

PAUL FOGGARTY. phone the peelers an tell them what we've found

HARRY FOGGARTY. are you out a yer fuckin mind – that's never goin to happen right – but tell me anyway what good would it do

PAUL FOGGARTY. we could find out what the story is

HARRY FOGGARTY. tell me this did ya love my da

PAUL FOGGARTY. don't be askin stupid fuckin questions

HARRY FOGGARTY. did ya or didn't ya

PAUL FOGGARTY. of course a did he was my da

HARRY FOGGARTY. right – i loved him too – and now he's dead

PAUL FOGGARTY. and what

HARRY FOGGARTY. say it's the worst which it's not – say my da did shoot somebody and they're dead – and now he's dead – what – it goin to bring whoever he shot back to life – no – all that's goin to happen is that the world's goin to know that my da shot someone and he's not around to tell anybody why

PAUL FOGGARTY. yer tellin me ya don't want to know why

HARRY FOGGARTY. a don't need to know why because a already do know – a know my da was a hard workin strict wee man who did the best he could at a time when things here were fucked up – and a don't know about any a this but a do know he wasn't a bad man – ya wanted to do something for yer da – plant some flowers for him – i'll tell ya what to do for him – bury these an say fuck all about

PAUL FOGGARTY. i don't like this

HARRY FOGGARTY. neither do i – grab a shovel

PAUL FOGGARTY. i'm not doin it – i'm not getting involved – fuck it leave them there

HARRY FOGGARTY. you do what you want but i know what i've to do (*He lifts a shovel.*) what are ya standin there for go on fuck off

10

The shop. BETTY *is behind the counter. She is wearing her new dress.* BOP *is hesitant about what he is about to do.*

BETTY LENNON. yer the last one – just made it in time – about to close up it's been a long day

BOP TORBETT. aye

SAMMY LENNON (*from upstairs*). this is nearly ready betty

BETTY LENNON. i've a customer – i'm closin up after that

SAMMY LENNON. right i'll not put the soup out yet then

BETTY LENNON (*to* BOP). think he ran a swanky restaurant to hear him

BOP TORBETT. this bottle of water (*Hand in his pocket pretending he has a gun.*) don't move – it's a joke right – don't move

BETTY LENNON. take it easy son – it's alright – ya can take what ya want – don't shoot me

BOP TORBETT (*takes his hand out of his pocket*). a don't have anything – look nothing – i'm sorry – a don't know why i'm doin this – i'm sorry

BOP *exits.*

SAMMY LENNON (*from upstairs.*) everything alright down there

BETTY LENNON. yes – it's alright

Silence. BETTY *takes the club from under the counter and starts smashing the place up.*

11

A house. JOE *is just home.* MAEVE *is in another room.*

JOE HYNES. maeve

MAEVE HYNES. i'm out here

JOE HYNES. what's the cot doin here – we can't afford to buy that wee girl a cot

MAEVE HYNES. a got a lend of it

JOE HYNES. what for

MAEVE *enters with the baby in her arms.*

MAEVE HYNES. somewhere for this wee man to sleep

JOE HYNES. what the fuck

MAEVE HYNES. before ya say anythin joe just listen

JOE HYNES. there's nothin that you can say maeve that's goin to make this

MAEVE HYNES. it's not what ya think

JOE HYNES. it's what a think alright ya crazy bitch

MAEVE HYNES. don't say that – listen – i know a shouldn't have done this – stealin something isn't right

JOE HYNES. isn't right – you'll get fuckin locked up for this

MAEVE HYNES. a thought if we had somethin of our own to look after for a while

JOE HYNES. of our own – you've taken someone else's baby – ya crazy fucker – is it yer cousin's

MAEVE HYNES. it's not hers

JOE HYNES. do ya not see what you've done here

MAEVE HYNES. do you want me to explain

JOE HYNES. no i don't want you to fuckin explain – a want somebody to come and take you away an put ya in a fuckin straitjacket – i've had enough i'm not doin this any more

MAEVE HYNES. what are ya not doin any more joe

JOE HYNES. jesus christ – have children – anybody who would do something like that maeve isn't fit to be a mother – don't think too i'm goin to help ya i'm not – i'll sign any fuckin report or anythin that says yer not right in the head – selfish fuckin bitch

MAEVE HYNES. what is it yer not goin to do any more joe

JOE HYNES. i'm not pretendin – pretendin that our life together isn't a sham – pretendin to be interested in the crap ya talk about our future together – pretendin what a do everyday is worth all this – pretendin a like comin home when a want to be somewhere else – and the big one – pretending yer in some way fuckin normal and that i still love you

MAEVE HYNES. not normal

JOE HYNES. better fuckin believe it's not normal

MAEVE *lets the baby fall to the floor.*

MAEVE HYNES. it's a dummy joe it's not real – the let mothers-to-be practise on them – i stole one of them because i thought that if you and i could spend a weekend pretending to look after a child of our own that it might make you want one the way i did – that we could both want something together – that's all joe – nothing more than that – nothing crazy just something to bring us together – it felt like that's what we needed – but you have other plans – somewhere else you want to be – to be with someone else

MAEVE *lifts the baby up and puts it in the cot.*

when did it start – it doesn't matter i don't care – no a do – was it before or after i found out about – my – difficulty in having a child

JOE HYNES. maeve

MAEVE HYNES. before or after

JOE HYNES. before

MAEVE HYNES. i don't know why but that makes me feel a bit better

JOE HYNES. what are we going to do

MAEVE HYNES. we – what are we going to do – i'm not going to do anythin joe – you've just told me what ya thought of me – what can i do

JOE HYNES. a didn't mean things to happen this way

MAEVE HYNES. what way did ya mean them to happen –
that i would never know and you could go on pretending –
or maybe i was to find somethin in yer pocket – somethin to
give the game away and i was to confront ya – and some-
how it would all turn round that it's my fault – and although
i wasn't happy with the situation i would feel a bit guilty
about it all – so i would forgive you – and we could go
through the rest of our lives me thinking what's wrong with
me – what is it about me that makes my husband want to
fuck other women – and you thinkin these things happen –
that's the way of the world – is that the way ya meant it to
happen – jesus – a thought just came to me there – i know
who it is – a don't know her but a saw her – kept lookin at
me that whole time i was in the shop – this girl kept lookin
at me then if i caught her eye she'd look away – she runs
the pub or somethin – it's her isn't it

JOE HYNES. no

MAEVE HYNES. doesn't matter – it is though i know it is

JOE HYNES. do ya want me to explain

MAEVE HYNES. don't say a damn thing – i'm not givin ya
the chance to justify yerself that's not goin to happen – you
hurt me joe an that's it – that's all ya need to understand –
funny thing i feel in some way – lighter – when a was up at
the hospital today lookin at all those babies i kept thinkin
maybe joe an i aren't right for havin children – that was the
first time a thought that – i think that's why a brought the doll
home – to give us a chance to prove me wrong – ya can take
one of the good suitcases – i'll iron some clothes for you

JOE HYNES. that mightn't be what a want

MAEVE HYNES. ya don't have a choice joe – i'm doin my
best to maintain what little dignity i have left – if you were
to stay here joe i'd only end up havin to cut yer fuckin eyes
out – a wouldn't be pretendin either

12

The pub. HELEN *is behind the bar.* FRANK *is sitting on his own as is* SHARON. *Her suitcase is on top of the table.* SHANKS *is at the bar paying for a carryout. Both him and* SHARON *are drunk.*

SHANKS O'NEILL (*puts all his change on the counter*). if there's anythin left out a that just give me it in tins – (*To* SHARON.) alright there dear

SHARON LAWTHER. aye

SHANKS O'NEILL. ya drink tins don't ya

SHARON LAWTHER. tins aye

SHANKS O'NEILL (*to* HELEN). – out of a shitty poe she'd drink it

HELEN WOODS. ya takin her home

SHANKS O'NEILL. me an her – don't worry she'll be alright – i'll look after her

HELEN WOODS. do that

SHANKS O'NEILL. a will – a will – ya know me – i'm the man for lookin after the women (*To* SHARON.) right come on dear let's hit the road – what's in that suitcase ya have

SHARON LAWTHER. nothin

SHANKS O'NEILL. put the tins in it – easier carried

Puts tins in suitcase.

SHARON LAWTHER. tins in a suitcase – let's go

SHANKS O'NEILL (*to* FRANK). cheers

FRANK COIN. good luck

SHANKS *exits.*

SHARON LAWTHER (*to* HELEN). ya want a piece of advice dear

HELEN WOODS. what's that

SHARON LAWTHER. all men are a shower a shite

SHARON *exits*.

HELEN WOODS. think they'll make it

FRANK COIN. ya wouldn't know – people always seem to find their way home no matter what

HELEN WOODS. it's findin their way back here i'm worried about

HELEN *pours them both a drink. She sits at the counter and lights a cigarette. She holds the lighter flicking the lid open and closed.*

FRANK COIN. good health

HELEN WOODS. have a few drinks before a close up

FRANK COIN. it's nearly that time alright – nice lighter

HELEN WOODS. aye (*Hands it to him.*)

FRANK COIN. used to have one like it myself

HELEN WOODS. didn't know ya smoked

FRANK COIN. used to – my wife elsie bought it for me

HELEN WOODS. how long's she dead now frank

FRANK COIN. ten years nearly eleven

HELEN WOODS. long time

FRANK COIN. feels like no time sometimes and others it's like a lifetime

HELEN WOODS. she smoke did she

FRANK COIN. the two of us – like chimneys – that's what killed her – a stopped then (*Hands lighter back.*)

JOE *is at home sitting at a table. He is smoking a cigarette. He makes a phone call.* HELEN*'s mobile rings.* JOE *walks into the scene.* HELEN *lets the phone ring then she switches it off.* JOE *exits.*

not want to hear what the have to say

HELEN WOODS. no a don't

FRANK COIN. boyfriend is it

HELEN WOODS. used to be – a realised he wasn't the man for me when he stopped smokin

FRANK COIN. better off without him – married men can be difficult

HELEN WOODS. what do you mean married men

FRANK COIN. can't get away with anythin round here – the mightn't say it but nearly everybody knows nearly everythin

HELEN WOODS. people talkin about it were the

FRANK COIN. sure who'd be talkin to me – i'm either listenin to the radio out walkin or in here – there's days the only voice a hear is my own – there'll be other men for ya

HELEN WOODS. a hope not

FRANK COIN. it's the company of somebody that puts the smile on yer face

HELEN WOODS. men are all a shower a shite you heard her – thinkin of takin myself off somewhere

FRANK COIN. on holidays

HELEN WOODS. a don't know – maybe for good

FRANK COIN. yer young enough to be doin it – don't leave it too long

HELEN WOODS. you lived round here all yer life aye

FRANK COIN. most of it – come up from the country to work – got married – elsie was from round here so that was that – out where i'm from there's no one left – this is home now – a used to think about movin back when there was ones alive – sure ya think these things but never do them – there's worse places than this

HELEN WOODS. ya want another drink

FRANK COIN. i'll finish this that's that – enough's plenty

HELEN WOODS. ya ordered yer taxi or do ya want me to do it

FRANK COIN. i'm goin walk home tonight a think – know what a heard on the radio this mornin – there's goin to be a meteorite storm tonight – light the whole sky up the said – there was another fella sayin that it was the beginnin of the end of the world – people talk a lot of balls don't the

HELEN WOODS. aye – he didn't say when the end was did he

FRANK COIN. no he did not – that's a more difficult one – the radio's a great thing – there was another fella on – this programme was all about space – he said that when we talk – the sound we make travels up into space and goes on forever – it never goes away

HELEN WOODS. some of the things i've said frank a want them to go away

FRANK COIN. listenin to it a had this thought y'know – wouldn't it be good to think that if there was somebody ya could no longer talk too – that if ya said somethin to them that yer words would travel up into space and that the might meet up with words that that person had once said to you – wouldn't that be a nice thing

HELEN WOODS. it would frank

FRANK COIN. right i'll finish this then that's me for the day

HELEN WOODS. you'll be back tomorrow

FRANK COIN. a will

13

The street. MAGGIE *is standing alone.* BOP *arrives. They sit on the pavement.*

MAGGIE LYTTLE. where were you

BOP TORBETT. nowhere – just walkin about – ya not go to the club

MAGGIE LYTTLE. didn't feel like it – what happened round

at the shop

BOP TORBETT. nothin

MAGGIE LYTTLE. ya didn't get the skins then

BOP TORBETT. no

MAGGIE LYTTLE (*produces joint*). have to smoke this then

BOP TORBETT. where'd ya get that

MAGGIE LYTTLE. swiz had skins

They smoke the joint.

BOP TORBETT. those two laughin at me for not comin back were the

MAGGIE LYTTLE. what the fuck do you care – are swiz an cooper here – no – am i here – yes – this is yer last chance bop

BOP TORBETT. yer very bossy

MAGGIE LYTTLE. i am not

BOP TORBETT. are so

MAGGIE LYTTLE. arsehole

BOP TORBETT. today was shit ya know that

MAGGIE LYTTLE. even the jacuzzi

BOP TORBETT. what jacuzzi ya kiddin me – she knocked swiz back an then threw the two of us out – a should've went swimmin shouldn't a

MAGGIE LYTTLE. yes

BOP TORBETT. i hate this place

MAGGIE *lies back and looks up at the sky.*

we'll go swimmin tomorrow

MAGGIE LYTTLE. teach you to be a fish

FRANK COIN *walks past.*

14

FRANK *stops in the street and looks up at the sky. He is surrounded by noise. A baby crying. A busy road. Loud music. Church bells ringing. Heavy machinery, Police sirens. Gun shots. People arguing. Screaming.* BOP TORBETT *and* MAGGIE LYTTLE *are lying on the pavement. In the sky there is a meteorite storm. The stage is covered in a brilliant white light. The stage begins to darken and the noise dies.*

FRANK COIN (*looking up at the sky*). i miss you elsie

The stage darkens to black. A sonar bleep in the night sky.